Great Le Words of Wisdom

Over 1000 Quotations on Great Leadership
from global business leaders, statesmen,
athletes, coaches, sages,
and philosophers.

Steven B. Howard

Great Leadership Words of Wisdom

ISBN: 978-1-943702-68-8 (Print edition)
    978-1-943702-76-3 (Kindle edition)

Published by:
Caliente Press
1775 E Palm Canyon Drive, Suite 110-198
Palm Springs, CA 92264
U.S.A.
Email: steven@CalientePress.com

Cover Design: Zachery Colman

Contents

Introduction 9

Leadership 13

Quotes on Leadership 21

Leadership Philosophy 37

Quotes on Leadership Philosophy 41

Leadership Mindset 53

Leading Teams and People 71

Leading People Development 97

Quotes on Leading People Development 103

Leading Employee Engagement 115

Quotes on Leading Employee Engagement 121

Leading For Results 135

Ensuring Accountability 159

Leadership Mindfulness 189

Leading Your Own Personal Development 209

Steven Howard's Personal Leadership Philosophy 231

Steven Howard's Rules of Great Leadership 233

About the Author 237

Dedication

This book is dedicated to

Ed & Angel

My first bosses.

Your impact on my life was greater than you knew.

Success comes from knowing that you did your best to become the best that you are capable of becoming.

John Wooden

Introduction

Quotations have always had the power to inspire me.

When I was a child I started a collection of quotes on 3x5 index cards and kept these safely tucked away in my own personal plastic box.

Later, when I moved to Asia as an adult I started collecting quotes from Asian philosophers, sages, and leaders. This collection was published in my *Asian Words of Wisdom* series of quote books, which now numbers five titles in print.

When I first started collection quotations, sayings, and proverbs, I was simply impressed by the pure logic or the stupefying memorability of a good quote.

Today, while the fascination with quotes remains, I am now more enthralled by the thinking and background behind each impressive saying I come across. I am equally absorbed by reflecting on the relevance and motivational aspects of these quotes in today's world.

I hope you will take time to reflect upon the words and thoughts on great leadership in this book. I also hope that the ideas found within this book will provide inspiration and motivation for your own personal growth and development as a leader.

This book is structured around my belief that great leadership is an art.

It is the art of achieving progress through the involvement and actions of others. This is why great leaders are strong in both leading people and leading for results, while good or mediocre leaders typically focus their leadership efforts on only one or the other.

Having conducted leadership development programs for over 10,000 mid-level leaders, supervisors, new managers, and senior leaders in Asia, Australia, Africa, Europe, North America, and the South Pacific I can attest to the critical importance of leaders placing focus on both leading people and leading for results in creating sustainable success.

This is why I created my 8 Keys to Great Leadership model:

Personal Leadership Philosophy

Leadership Mindset

Core Set of Leadership Behaviors Aligned With The Organization's Culture

Leading Teams and People

Leading People Development

Leading For Results

Ensuring Accountability

Communicating as a Leader

The results from developing leadership skills in these eight key areas of great leadership include performance enhancement, better leveraging and utilization of existing leadership skills, enhanced communications as a leader, increased team member engagement, and greater consistency in leadership behaviors congruent with the organization's brand and culture.

I am sure you will find many nuggets of useful wisdom within these pages that are relevant to your current or future leadership challenges and desires.

My best wishes for your continued success.

Steven B. Howard
December 2017

CHAPTER 1

Leadership

L eadership is not a sometime thing, it's an all-the-time thing. You cannot lead every now and then, or only when the urge to lead hits you

Leaders have to lead all the time. Leadership is a collection of skills that become habitual behaviors, either consciously or unconsciously. Great leadership is a deliberate, conscious, and purposeful habit. So too, unfortunately, is the failure to lead.

The old school of leadership is just that — old school. Gone are the days of Control and Command leaders in the workplace. And, to a lesser degree, gone too are the days of dominant personality leadership.

Sure, there are exceptions to these changes. But for the most part critical leadership skills have segued into a focus on behaviors and actions over traits, titles, and "looking the part." As today's pithy saying goes, *you don't have to have a title to be a leader.*

Leadership is not a position, title, or spot on an organizational chart. Leadership is a skill to be developed, practiced, and enhanced.

This focus on the behaviors and actions of leaders is often paired with an understanding that leaders are made, not born, and that anyone, at any level within an organization, can be a leader.

One of the key challenges facing leaders is knowing when to be a leader, and when to be a manager. Management and leadership each comprise a set of distinct behavioral skills and responsibilities. These are not style changes or personality traits that can be flipped on and off like a light switch.

As Linda E. Ginzel, clinical professor of managerial psychology at the University of Chicago Booth School of Management wrote, *"Recognize that what matters is not whether you fit into some leadership suit of clothes or match up to some template of a leader personality. What matters is how you choose to behave."*

Adds Roger Trapp, in an article in *Forbes*, *"This distinction is crucial because, unlike traits, behaviors form the basis for skills, and skills can be practiced."* Additionally, skills can be developed and learned.

Managing vs. Leading

A leadership role is significantly different from a manager role.

These differences may have been best summarized by leading management thinker Peter Drucker, *"Managers do things right. Leaders do the right things."* Add to this the wisdom of Klaus Balkenhol, a gold-medal winning Olympian, *"There is a difference between being a leader and being a boss. Both are based on authority. A boss demands blind obedience; a leader earns his authority through understanding and trust."*

Another distinction is that managers will say "go do this" to their subordinates, whereas leaders will be heard saying "let's go do this."

For those in first-line or first-time supervisory and leadership positions, one of the hardest tasks is juggling and switching between these managerial and leadership activities and responsibilities. Most such leaders are required to alternate hats between moments when they need to use managerial behaviors and when they need to perform as a leader.

This balancing act is further complicated if they also have their own individual contributor responsibilities to deliver.

New leaders also tend to cling and hold onto projects and responsibilities longer than necessary, often thinking that doing so shows they are a hard worker and worthy of future promotion. A good leader cannot afford to hold onto projects and programs after they have achieved initial objectives. Their time is better spent on move important issues, including people development, strategy planning, and driving innovation.

Great leaders are constantly focused on future opportunities and challenges, instead of relishing past accomplishments and reminding others of what they have achieved in the past.

While managers are rightfully focused on tasks, processes, procedures, and policies, leaders need to additionally concentrate on the people aspect of the business. As U.S. Navy Rear Admiral Grace Murray Hopper stated, *"You manage things. You lead people."*

We would add that leaders, especially great leaders, also lead people development, a topic we will cover in more detail in chapter five.

Going from being a manager to becoming a leader is all about mindset...where you place your focus and attention...and whether your mental focus is placed on getting things done or about leading people to achieve results.

This requires an emphasis on six critical leadership behaviors that impact sustainable success for any organization:

Leading People and Teams

Leading for Results

Ensuring Accountability

Communicating as a Leader

Leading Employee Engagement

Leading Continuous People Development

These six leadership focus areas are the keys to creating a high-performing climate for whichever portion of the organization you lead.

Many research studies have proven that leaders who create positive workplace climates achieve more stellar results than leaders who do not. One of the most cited of such studies, by the Hay Group, showed that:

A positive climate will increase results by up to 30%.

A poor climate is virtually a guarantee of poor performance.

50% to 70% of the variance in organizational climate can be explained by differences in leadership styles.

It is also well documented that the maxim "people leave bosses, not organizations" is excruciatingly true. Unfortunately, this results in tremendous costs to organizations to replace good employees who leave due to the unsatisfying climate they find in their departments and work teams.

Results Focus or People Focus?

You may now be asking yourself, are great leaders more focused on results or people? Which makes the better leader, a no-nonsense, drive-home-the-results type or the motivational, let's-put-people-first style?

Well, in 2009 James Zenger published an extraordinary study of 60,000 employees in an attempt to answer this question. His survey was designed to identify if different characteristics of a leader affected whether employees perceived the leader as a great leader or not.

The results of this study were astonishing and crystal clear. If a leader was perceived by his or her staff as being strongly results focused, then that leader was seen as a great leader only 14% of the time. Likewise, if a leader was perceived by his or staff as being strongly focused on people, then that leader was seen as a great leader only 12% of the time.

However, those leaders who displayed a balanced approach and focus on both results and people were perceived as great leaders a phenomenal 72% of the time. So the answer to the question of results focus vs. people focus is not either one or the other, but clearly a combination of both. This has certainly been true of the great leaders I have worked under, consulted, or coached.

Great leaders know full well that performance results and change implementation are actually best derived from the engagement and motivation of team members, particularly those who receive continuous skill development.

As Marilyn Hewson succinctly puts it, *"Good leaders organize and align people around what the team needs to do. Great leaders motivate and inspire people with why they're doing it. That's purpose. And that's the key to achieving something truly transformational."*

The best leaders are people who lead from their own personal strengths, leadership philosophy, and leadership mindset. Great leaders also understand that organizational energy, workplace synergy, and end results are best attained when ambitious people with different backgrounds and thinking preferences are allowed to perform work together in a safe and supportive environment.

Great leaders know how to create such successful and supportive climates by applying the skills of adaptability, motivation, coaching, focus, collaboration, decision-making, communications, and skill development to both themselves and the people they lead.

Our preferred definition of leadership is: *leadership is the art of achieving progress through the involvement and actions of others.*

Great leaders focus on four critical areas to increase employee engagement and drive performance results:

Giving team members a sense of purpose and a compelling context for committing to buy-in.

Granting team members appropriate levels of autonomy.

Showing empathy to team members by understanding the emotions and feelings they are going through, particularly during times of change.

Creating a safe environment where mistakes are tolerated (and learned from) and where accountability is fair and unbiased.

These four critical areas help leaders leverage the emotions of passion, enthusiasm, self-satisfaction, trust, and loyalty to drive creativity, thinking, innovation, energy, and buy-in to strategies, tactics, and activities in pursuit of clearly stated goals and objectives.

The Art of Great Leadership

It has often been said that "managers do things right while leaders do the right things." There's a great deal of truth in this pithy observation. Especially as my concept of great leadership is applied.

Managers should be responsible for ensuring appropriate implementation of policies, procedures, and processes. Great leaders, in addition to determining and communicating direction, are responsible for people leadership and people development. This includes leadership and development of themselves.

The art of great leadership mandates a positive and future-focus mindset. You will not find many successful leaders who are pessimistic. Nor are those focused solely on short-term results (such as quarterly revenue and profit figures) likely to be successful over the long term.

This does not mean leadership requires wearing rose-colored glasses or having an unrealistic view that all will become right soon.

Rather, the art of great leadership requires a solid grounding in both understanding the reality of any situation, while simultaneously being able to integrate various viewpoints of reality that they and others hold. This means both understanding the status quo and being able to question the underlining nature of the status quo, and how this is perceived and believed by others.

Leaders also have to inspire confidence in the organization and its sustainable future.

Some leaders are born to lead. Most leaders are created by circumstances, aptitude, and an internal willingness or drive to lead others.

The thing is: *anyone at any level of an organization can be a great leader.*

With a succinct personal leadership philosophy (see chapter two) and a strong leadership mindset (see chapter three), combined with a purposeful set of leadership behaviors, you can develop into a leader of which you will be proud.

Great leadership is not something reserved for senior management, business owners, and entrepreneurs. Anyone can be a great leader, if only of themselves. One does not need direct reports or to head a multi-functional team to be a great leader.

As such, anyone can implement the art of great leadership and the skills of great leadership.

Quotes on Leadership

Those who have high thoughts are ever striving; they are not happy to remain in the same place.
Buddha

I studied the lives of great men and famous women, and I found that the men and women who got to the top were those who did the jobs they had in hand, with everything they had of energy and enthusiasm and hard work.
Harry S. Truman

Failing organizations are usually over-managed and under-led.
Warren Bennis

Leadership is action, not position.
Donald H. McGannon

The fellow who doesn't need a boss is often selected to be one.
Christopher Morley

How you do one thing is how you do everything.
Zen Proverb

You can lead without character, but character is what makes you a leader worth following.
Andy Stanley

Your gifts are not about you. Leadership is not about you. Your purpose is not about you. A life of significance is about <u>serving</u> those who need your gifts, your leadership, your purpose.
Kevin Hall

The leader acts as though everyone is watching even when no one is watching.
Brian Tracy

If your actions inspire others to dream more, learn more, do more and become more, you are a leader.
John Quincy Adams

I'm their leader, I've got to follow them.
Alexandre Ledru-Rollin

The most reliable way to anticipate the future is by understanding the present.
John Naisbitt

Take action every day — some small dose at a time.
Jeffrey Gitomer

Leadership is a combination of strategy and character. If you must be without one, be without the strategy.
General H. Norman Schwarzkopf

A leader is a dealer in hope.
Napoleon Bonaparte

Setting an example is not the main means of influencing others; it is the only means.
Albert Einstein

Every political leader worth their salt in history — from Gandhi to Martin Luther King — has expressed the same message, which is courage. Real leaders don't tell people to be frightened. They help people find a place of courage, even in the face of very real threats.
Naomi Klein

If you just set out to be liked, you will be prepared to compromise on anything at any time, and would achieve nothing.
Margaret Thatcher

To value oneself and, at the same time, subordinate oneself to higher purposes and principles is the paradoxical essence of the highest humanity and the foundation of effective leadership.
Stephen Covey

Vision is the spectacular that inspires us to carry out the mundane.
Chris Widener

The only limit to our realization of tomorrow will be our doubts of today.
Franklin D. Roosevelt

Leadership is the art of getting someone else to do something you want done because he wants to do it.
Dwight D. Eisenhower

In any moment of decision, the best thing you can do is the right thing. The worst thing you can do is nothing.
Theodore Roosevelt

Most people spend more time and energy going around problems than in trying to solve them.
Henry Ford

Only three things happen naturally in organizations: friction, confusion, and underperformance. Everything else requires leadership.
Peter Drucker

Real leaders are ordinary people with extraordinary determinations.
John Seaman Garns

A clear vision, backed by definite plans, gives you a tremendous feeling of confidence and personal power.
Brian Tracy

Some attributes of leadership are universal and are often about finding ways of encouraging people to combine their efforts, their talents, their insights, their enthusiasm, and their inspiration to work together.
Queen Elizabeth II

What it lies in our power to do, it lies in our power not to do.
Aristotle

Leadership is not about titles, positions, or flow charts. It is about one life influencing another.
John Maxwell

Being responsible sometimes means pissing people off.
Colin Powell

There is a difference between being a leader and being a boss. Both are based on authority. A boss demands blind obedience; a leader earns his authority through understanding and trust.
Klaus Balkenhol

The very essence of leadership is that you have to have vision. You can't blow an uncertain trumpet.
Father Theodore M. Hesburgh

When eagles are silent, parrots begin to chatter.
Winston Churchill

A leader takes people where they would never go on their own.
Hans Finzel

A man who wants to lead the orchestra must turn his back on the crowd.
Max Lucado

Anyone can hold the helm when the sea is calm.
Publilius Syrus

People buy into the leader before they buy into the vision.
John Maxwell

Leadership is the capacity to translate vision into reality.
Warren Bennis

To have long-term success as a coach or in any position of leadership, you have to be obsessed in some way.
Pat Riley

Leadership is not a position, title, or spot on an organizational chart. Leadership is a skill to be developed, practiced, and enhanced.
Steven B. Howard

Success at the highest level comes down to one question: "Can you make the choice that your happiness can come from someone else's success?" No one has qualities like courage, vision, charisma, adaptability, and decisiveness in equal measure. But every great leader does make the same decision — and so can you.
Jeff Haden

Leaders think and talk about the solutions. Followers think and talk about the problems.
Brian Tracy

Leadership is the art of giving people a platform for spreading ideas that work.
Seth Godin

Leadership is the ability to hide your panic from others.
Lao-Tzu

I suppose leadership at one time meant muscles; but today it means getting along with people.
Mohandas Karamchand (Mahatma) Gandhi

You can preach a better sermon with your life than with your lips.
Oliver Goldsmith

You have to do what you think is right. If you don't, you are not a leader.
Ben Horowitz

In one spark of fire there is the whole fire. It can ignite whole cities and nations. One spark. That's how the truth of one person from age to age can shake the whole earth.
Swami Amar Jyoti

There is no greatness without a passion to be great, whether it's the aspiration of an athlete or an artist, a scientist, a parent or a business person.
Anthony Robbins

One person with a belief is equal to a force of ninety-nine with only interests.
John Stuart Mill

Nothing is more powerful for your future than being a gatherer of good ideas and information. That's called doing your homework.
Jim Rohn

Power lasts ten years; influence not more than a hundred.
Korean Proverb

Thinking is the hardest work there is, which is probably the reason so few engage in it.
Henry Ford

As you move into higher leadership positions, part of your net worth to your organization and to your team is your network.
Steven B. Howard

A leader is best when people barely know he exists, when his work is done, his aim fulfilled, they will say 'We did it ourselves.'
Lao-Tzu

The art of leadership is saying no, not yes. It is very easy to say yes.
Tony Blair

Become the kind of leader that people would follow voluntarily, even if you had no title or position.
Brian Tracy

Leadership should be more participative than directive, more enabling than performing.
Mary D. Poole

Vision is where tomorrow begins, for it expresses what you and others who share the vision will be working hard to create. Since most people don't take the time to think systematically about the future, those who do, and who base their strategies and actions on their visions, have inordinate power to shape the future.
Burt Nanus

You have to decide what your highest priorities are and have the courage — pleasantly, smilingly, non-apologetically — to say 'no' to other things. And the way you do that is by having a bigger 'yes' burning inside. The enemy of the 'best' is often the 'good.'
Stephen Covey

Don't follow the crowd, let the crowd follow you.
Margaret Thatcher

The more you sweat in peace, the less you bleed in war.
General H. Norman Schwarzkopf

The task of leadership is not to put greatness into humanity, but to elicit it, for the greatness is already there.
John Buchan

You cannot build a reputation on what you are going to do.
Henry Ford

One of the true tests of leadership is the ability to recognize a problem before it becomes an emergency.
Arnold Glasgow

The best way to predict the future is to invent it.
Alan Kay

Great crisis produce great men and great deeds of courage.
John F. Kennedy

As a leader, I am tough on myself and I raise the standard for everybody; however, I am very caring because I want people to excel at what they are doing so that they can aspire to be me in the future.
Indra Nooyi

Innovation distinguishes between a leader and a follower.
Steve Jobs

What you do has far greater impact than what you say.
Stephen Covey

Leading an organization is like frying a small fish. You spoil it with too much poking.
Lao-Tzu

To handle yourself, use your head; to handle others, use your heart.
Eleanor Roosevelt

No man will make a great leader who wants to do it all himself, or to get all the credit for doing it.
Andrew Carnegie

A leader, once convinced that a particular course of action is the right one, must be undaunted when the going gets rough.
Ronald Reagan

Opportunities for leadership are all around us. The capacity for leadership is deep within us.
Madeleine Albright

The man who knows how will always have a job. The man who knows why will always be his boss.
Ralph Waldo Emerson

He that would govern others, first should be The Master of himself.
Philip Massinger

No man is fit to command another that cannot command himself.
William Penn

Spend eighty percent of your time focusing on the opportunities of tomorrow rather than the problems of yesterday.
Brian Tracy

Do not wait for leaders. Do it alone, person to person.
Mother Teresa

A mediocre idea that generates enthusiasm will go further than a great idea that inspires no one.
Mary Kay Ash

Entrepreneurial leadership requires the ability to move quickly when opportunity presents itself.
Brian Tracy

Winners compare their achievements with their goals, while losers compare their achievements with those of other people.
Nido Qubein

Real leaders forever need bigger and more irresistible challenges.
Mark Victor Hansen

The task of an educated mind is simply put: read to lead.
Marcus Tullius Cicero

One of the advantages of being a leader is being able to ask for advice without necessarily having to follow it.
Steven B. Howard

A leader's role is to raise people's aspirations for what they can become and to release their energies so they will try to get there.
David Gergen

Leadership is the great challenge of the 21st century in science, politics, education, and industry. But the greatest challenge in leadership is parenting. We need to do more than just get our enterprises ready for the challenges of the 21st century. We also need to get our children ready for the challenges of the 21st century.
Jim Rohn

Do what you can to show you care about other people, and you will make our world a better place.
Rosalynn Carter

Reason and judgment are the qualities of a leader.
Publius Cornelius Tacitus

A good leader can never be a hypocrite.
Mohamed Amroussi

The art of being wise is the art of knowing what to overlook.
William James

The art of communication is the language of leadership.
James Humes

Happiness comes when your work and words are of benefit to yourself and others.
Buddha

Live, love, laugh, learn and lead by example. Those five things are, I believe, the basis of life.
Sean Swarner

I sit here all day trying to persuade people to do the things they ought to have sense enough to do without my persuading them.
Harry S. Truman

It takes 20 years to build a reputation and five minutes to ruin it. If you think about that, you'll do things differently.
Warren Buffett

I cannot trust a man to control others who cannot control himself.
Robert E. Lee

The day the soldiers stop bringing you their problems is the day you stopped leading them. They have either lost confidence that you can help them or concluded that you do not care. Either case is a failure of leadership.
Colin Powell

If you want to build a ship, don't drum up the men to gather wood, divide the work, and give orders. Instead, teach them to yearn for the vast and endless sea.
Antoine de Saint-Exupéry

Great leaders are almost always simplifiers, who can cut through argument, debate, and doubt to offer a solution everybody can understand.
Colin Powell

If more politicians in this country were thinking about the next generation instead of the next election, it might be better for the United States and the world.
Senator Claude Pepper

The final test of a leader is that he leaves behind him in other men the conviction and the will to carry on.
Walter Lippmann

Leadership is about making others better as a result of your presence and making sure that impact lasts in your absence.
Sheryl Sandberg

Leaders spend 5% of their time on the problem and 95% of their time on the solution. Get over it and crush it.
Anthony Robbins

Today a reader, tomorrow a leader.
Margaret Fuller

Leadership is not about men in suits. It is a way of life for those who know who they are and willing to be their best to create the life they want to live.
Kathleen Schafer

Good leaders organize and align people around what the team needs to do. Great leaders motivate and inspire people with why they're doing it. That's purpose. And that's the key to achieving something truly transformational.
Marilyn Hewson

I am endlessly fascinated that playing football is considered a training ground for leadership, but raising children isn't.
Dee Dee Myers

The leader is one who, out of clutter brings simplicity; out of discord, harmony; and out of difficulty, opportunity.
Albert Einstein

One voice can change a room.
Barack Obama

My job as a leader is to make sure everybody in the company has great opportunities, and that they feel they're having a meaningful impact.
Larry Page

Effective leadership is not about making speeches or being liked; leadership is defined by results, not attributes.
Peter Drucker

Leadership is not about a title or a designation. It's about impact, influence, and inspiration Impact involves getting results, influence is about spreading the passion you have for your work, and you have to inspire teammates and customers.
Robin S. Sharma

The signs of outstanding leadership appear primarily among the followers. Are the followers reaching their potential? Are they learning? Do they achieve the required results? Do they change with grace? Manage conflict?
Max De Pree

He who wishes to be obeyed must know how to command.
Niccolò Machiavelli

Your ability to solve problems and make good decisions is the true measure of your skill as a leader.
Brian Tracy

As a leader, it's a major responsibility on your shoulders to practice the behavior you want others to follow.
Himanshu Bhatia

The key to successful leadership today is influence, not authority.
Ken Blanchard

A leader is someone who demonstrates what is possible.
Mark Yarnell

Leadership is a two-way street, loyalty up and loyalty down. Respect for one's superiors; care for one's crew.
Rear Admiral Grace Murray Hopper

A leader leads by example not by force.
Sun Tzu

CHAPTER 2

Leadership Philosophy

One of the most important foundations for great leaders is having an understanding of their own leadership platform — a set of beliefs, values, and personal rules related to the kind of leader they want to be.

A leadership philosophy is a set of beliefs and principles that strongly influences how you interpret reality and guides how you react to people, events, and situations. Research has shown that consistent leadership behavior and actions require a clear personal leadership philosophy.

Konosuke Matsushita, the founder of Panasonic in Japan, is known in that country as the "god of management" for his writings and speeches on leadership and management. He wrote, *"If you are a leader, you must have an ideology of leadership. If you lack an ideology, and attempt to decide everything on a case-by-case basis, you will never be capable of strong leadership."*

A written leadership philosophy helps leaders demonstrate and communicate to team members and others what they expect, what they value, and how they will act in any given situation. This helps to make their workplace environment less stressful and more productive, as well as keeping them on track and aligned with their core beliefs and values.

Having a written personal leadership philosophy is one of the distinctions between great leaders and average leaders.

While a leadership philosophy is a set of core beliefs and principles about leadership and the type of leader you want to be, a leadership mindset, though closely related, is different. A leadership mindset is a set of core values upon which leadership behaviors are based (see chapter three).

Integrating these two sets of beliefs creates a foundation that will drive the organizational environment and climate of the team a leader leads, whether this is a four-person department or a multinational company with tens of thousands of employees.

Combining consistent behavioral actions with a personal leadership philosophy creates *great leadership*. These are the leaders who not only get results, but do so while building and enhancing the climate of their respective organizations, continuously developing the skills of themselves and their team members, and simultaneously creating new leaders (not just followers).

When a leader is consistent, they are able to inspire trust; whereas an inconsistent leader causes confusion, anxiety, angst, and uncertainty within their troops.

Developing Your Personal Leadership Philosophy

There are many ways to create your own personal leadership philosophy and leadership mindset. You could have your own set of rules, your own overriding philosophy of what is right, or know how you will act under pressure and changing circumstances. Or some combination of all three.

No single leadership philosophy can be viable for everyone. Each leader is faced with different circumstances, brings different backgrounds to their leadership positions, and leads widely different teams of people. Hence you have to figure out what the right leadership philosophy and mindset is for you.

Stop and ask yourself, "What is your personal leadership philosophy?" When was the last time you paused and seriously gave this question sufficient reflection? There's no time like the present to give this question some serious thought and consideration.

There are seven sets of questions to ask yourself in developing, reviewing, or fine-tuning your personal leadership philosophy:

> What is the primary focus of your leadership beliefs — results, people, both? Why?

> What do you want to accomplish in your current leadership role and as your career advances? Why?

> How would you like others to describe your leadership style and behaviors? With what specific words and terms?

> What do you expect from those you lead? How will you demonstrate and communicate this?

> What level of control makes you comfortable? What level of delegation makes you comfortable? Why?

> How do you view the mistakes of others? Of yourself? Why?

> What are your personal rules of leadership? Are these written down? Are these rigid or flexible?

For your reference, I have shared my personal rules of great leadership in the appendix at the end of this book. These are instrumental components of my personal leadership philosophy, which is at the heart of everything I write and teach about leadership:

> *Great leadership is an art.*
> *It is the art of achieving progress through*
> *the involvement and actions of others.*

Great leaders perform this art, and attain desired results, by having a personal leadership philosophy, the right leadership mindset, and through using the right tools and techniques. They are also consistent in their leadership behaviors.

Leadership Behaviors

Where do most of us learn our parenting skills? Usually from our own parents, and the parents of our spouse.

The same holds true for learning leadership skills. For most of us, this comes from observing the leaders and managers we have worked for or observed in action. We tend to cherry-pick the skills of those leaders that we personally liked, and pledge not to repeat the behaviors that we considered to be mistakes, irritations, or distasteful.

There are two problems with this approach.

First, if the behaviors of the leaders we have worked with and observed over time have been more hands-on managerial in nature, then we will likely exhibit similar tendencies. Secondly, we are making decisions based on behaviors that we personally like or prefer, without taking into account if these behaviors are best suited for the team members that we lead.

You can overcome these issues by contemplating your own leadership philosophy and the skill sets and leadership behaviors required to remain in alignment with your beliefs and values.

By creating and maintaining your own leadership philosophy and mindset, and then identifying the behaviors that will help you implement these guiding principles, you will avoid the trap highlighted by Konosuke Matsushita of deciding everything on a case-by-case basis. This results in consistency of leadership behavior; a benefit for both you and your team members.

Quotes on Leadership Philosophy

Vision without action is daydream. Action without vision is a nightmare.
Japanese Proverb

Don't judge each day by the harvest you reap, but by the seeds you plant.
Robert Louis Stevenson

Do what you feel in your heart to be right – for you'll be criticized anyway. You'll be damned if you do, and damned if you don't.
Eleanor Roosevelt

Leaders don't create followers, they create more leaders.
Tom Peters

Earn your leadership every day.
Michael Jordan

Live with integrity in the moment of choice.
Stephen Covey

An idea that is developed and put into action is more important than an idea that exists only as an idea.
Buddha

We yield on the side of making our people proud. It galvanizes our organization.
Howard Schultz

To be trusted is a greater compliment than to be loved.
George MacDonald

The greatest obstacle to discovery is not ignorance, it is the illusion of knowledge.
Daniel J. Boorstin

If you have the courage to begin, you have the courage to succeed.
David Viscott

Power is the ability to do good things for others.
Brooke Astor

The more you lose yourself in something bigger than yourself, the more energy you will have.
Norman Vincent Peale

The best reason to start an organization is to make meaning; to create a product or service to make the world a better place.
Guy Kawasaki

If you don't have a competitive advantage, don't compete.
Jack Welch

If you set your goals ridiculously high and it's a failure, you will fail above everyone else's success.
James Cameron

Entrepreneurs average 3.8 failures before final success. What sets the successful ones apart is their amazing persistence.
Lisa M. Amos

If you are not willing to risk the usual, you will have to settle for the ordinary.
Jim Rohn

Stop chasing the money and start chasing the passion.
Tony Hsieh

All our dreams can come true if we have the courage to pursue them.
Walt Disney

Don't be afraid to give up the good to go for the great.
John D. Rockefeller

Outstanding people have one thing in common: an absolute sense of mission.
Zig Ziglar

The topic of leadership is a touchy one. A lot of leaders fail because they don't have the bravery to touch that nerve or strike that chord. Throughout my years, I haven't had that fear.
Kobe Bryant

Those who cannot change their minds cannot change anything.
George Bernard Shaw

Belief precedes all action.
James Allen

The man with a new idea is a crank, until the idea succeeds.
Mark Twain

Belief in oneself is incredibly infectious. It generates momentum, the collective force of which far outweighs any kernel of self-doubt that may creep in.
Aimee Mullins

Most of what we say and do is not essential. If you can eliminate it, you'll have more time, and more tranquility. Ask yourself at every moment, "is this necessary?"
Marcus Aurelius

I do not think that there is any other quality so essential to success of any kind as the quality of perseverance. It overcomes almost everything, even nature.
John D. Rockefeller

Inspiration exists, but it has to find you working.
Pablo Picasso

Decide upon your major definite purpose in life and then organize all your activities around it.
Brian Tracy

Screw it, let's do it!
Richard Branson

The time is always right to do what is right.
Martin Luther King Jr.

Companies go wrong when they play defense instead of trying to score.
Howard Schultz

Choose always the way that seems best, however rough it may be. Custom will soon render it easy and agreeable.
Pythagoras

People think focus means saying yes to the thing you've got to focus on. But that's not what it means at all. It means saying no to the hundred other good ideas that there are. You have to pick carefully.
Steve Jobs

Your chances of success in any undertaking can always be measured by your belief in yourself.
Robert Collier

Planning is bringing the future into the present so that you can do something about it now.
Alan Lakein

When it is obvious that the goals cannot be reached, don't adjust the goals, adjust the action steps.
Confucius

Don't base your desired outcome on income. Do some good.
Steven B. Howard

Have a bias toward action. Let's see something happen now. You can break that big plan into small steps and take the first step right way.
Indira Gandhi

By recording your dreams and goals on paper, you set in motion the process of becoming the person you most want to be. Put your future in good hands — your own.
Mark Victor Hansen

There are risks and costs to action. But they are far less than the long-range risks of comfortable inaction.
John F. Kennedy

The biggest reward for a thing well done is to have done it.
Voltaire

The possession of anything begins in the mind.
Bruce Lee

What you get by achieving your goals is not as important as what you become by achieving your goals.
Zig Ziglar

Intuition becomes increasingly valuable in the new information society precisely because there is so much data.
John Naisbitt

A man should conceive of a legitimate purpose in his heart, and set out to accomplish it. He should make this purpose the centralizing point of his thoughts.
James Allen

When you have too many top priorities, you effectively have no top priorities.
Stephen Covey

One's philosophy is not best expressed in words; it is expressed in the choices one makes...and the choices we make are ultimately our responsibility.
Eleanor Roosevelt

The thing that motivates me is a very common form of motivation. And that is, with other folks counting on me, it's so easy to be motivated.
Jeff Bezos

The quality of a person's life is in direct proportion to their commitment to excellence, regardless of their chosen field of endeavor.
Vince Lombardi

Unless commitment is made, there are only promises and hopes...but no plans.
Peter Drucker

Life is really simple, but we insist on making it complicated.
Confucius

Those who are sincerely humbled by their own accomplishments will go on to accomplish even greater things.
Ralph Marston

If you believe in what you stand for as an enterprise — and you're willing to admit vulnerability — you have a chance to come out the right way.
Howard Schultz

A business is simply an idea to make other people's lives better.
Richard Branson

No one is unflawed or perfect. Flaws are charming and likable. Accept your flaws. Admit your mistakes. Doing so will not hurt you. But their denial and cover-up will.
Steven B. Howard

Impossible is a word only to be found in the dictionary of fools.
Napoleon Bonaparte

I like to listen. I have learned a great deal from listening carefully. Most people never listen.
Ernest Hemingway

Institutions serve people, not the other way around. So as a servant-leader, I measure my success by the success of those whom I'm serving.
John Calipari

Rank does not confer privilege or give power. It imposes responsibility.
Peter Drucker

It ain't what you don't know that gets you into trouble. It's what you know for sure that just ain't so.
Samuel Langhorne Clemens (Mark Twain)

It is not so much what you believe in that matters, as the way in which you believe it and proceed to translate that belief into action.
Lin Yu-Tang

If you wish to be a leader you will be frustrated, for very few people wish to be led. If you aim to be a servant you will never be frustrated.
Frank F. Warren

Seek advice but use your own common sense.
Yiddish Proverb

Management is problem-oriented, leadership is opportunity-oriented.
Stephen Covey

The most important thing about power is to make sure you don't have to use it.
Edwin Land

As we look ahead into the next century, leaders will be those who empower others.
Bill Gates

No one who achieves success does so without the help of others. The wise and confident acknowledge this help with gratitude.
Alfred North Whitehead

The greatest leader is not necessarily the one who does the greatest things. He is the one that gets the people to do the greatest things.
Ronald Reagan

Management is doing things right; leadership is doing the right things.
Peter Drucker

I start with the premise that the function of leadership is to produce more leaders, not more followers.
Ralph Nader

A good leader is a person who takes a little more than his share of the blame and a little less than his share of the credit.
John Maxwell

Leadership is not bullying and leadership is not aggression. Leadership is the expectation that you can use your voice for good. That you can make the world a better place.
Sheryl Sandberg

Wisdom is not about knowing all the answers. Wisdom is asking the right questions of the right person or people.
Steven B. Howard

Most people do not listen with the intent to understand; they listen with the intent to reply.
Stephen Covey

Solving problems means listening.
Richard Branson

The first responsibility of a leader is to define reality. The last is to say thank you. In between, the leader is a servant.
Max De Pree

As we look ahead into the next century, leaders will be those who empower others.
Bill Gates

I am not building a stock. I'm trying to build a great, enduring company.
Howard Schultz

Every leader needs to remember that a healthy respect for authority takes time to develop. It's like building trust. You don't instantly have trust, it has to be earned.
Mike Krzyzewski

CHAPTER 3

Leadership Mindset

*K**now thyself.*

Those words, inscribed in gold letters on the temple of Apollo at Delphi, are probably the most important two-word phrase ever written.

Knowing one's self has three components and combined they comprise three of the most important characteristics of great leaders: self-awareness, self-understanding, and self-esteem.

Self-awareness is a heightened sense of continuous attention to one's feelings, emotions, and thoughts. This is something all leaders should do, with particular attention paid to the word continuous.

Self-awareness is not about looking deep into your internal chamber of secrets trying to discover "your true self." Rather, it is an open, honest, candid, and on-going observation of what drives you to take the actions you take, to think the thoughts you have, and to feel the emotions that bubble up inside you.

Leaders with high levels of self-awareness have a clear and definite grasp of their own strengths and weaknesses, as well as an elevated sense of what motivates, de-motivates, satisfies, delights, annoys, and angers them.

Self-understanding is taking the awareness described above and grasping how your feelings, emotions, and thoughts are impacting your actions, behaviors, and decisions. If self-awareness is like putting your foot into a lake to see how cold the water is, self-understanding is diving into the lake to determine its depth.

The ancient Chinese philosopher Lao-Tzu placed great emphasis on self-understanding, writing, "*He who knows others is learned; he who knows himself is wise.*"

A keen sense of self-understanding, based on contemplation and reflection, will help you become authentic and remain authentic in the large majority of your actions. Only through a thorough understanding of yourself can you become truly authentic.

Dr. Nathaniel Branden, a Canadian psychotherapist and writer well known for his work in the psychology of self-esteem, wrote: "*Persons of high self-esteem are not driven to make themselves superior to others; they do not seek to prove their value by measuring themselves against a comparative standard. Their joy is being who they are, not in being better than someone else.*"

Another of Branden's insights is that, "*Self-esteem is the reputation that we acquire within ourselves.*" Think about that for a moment. You probably know what your reputation is amongst your friends, acquaintances, colleagues, and family members. But what is your reputation with yourself and of yourself?

These three characteristics are the DNA to how you formulate your leadership mindset.

Leadership Mindset

Writing in Psychology Today, Dr. Jim Taylor defines mindset as, "the attitudes, beliefs, and expectations you hold that act as the foundation of what you are, how you lead, and the ways in which you interact with your team."

He goes on in his article to explain, "Your mindset is so influential because it determines how you think about and interpret situations, your emotional reactions, the decisions you make, and the actions you take. Your mindset directly impacts the quality of your relationships, the interactions you have, and the way you lead. It also sets the tone for your organization and determines the kind of experiences your people have in their working lives."

A leadership mindset thus is a core set of personal values upon which the leader's behaviors, reactions, decisions, and actions are based. Your leadership mindset needs to be based on your beliefs and principles, how you view situations and people, your vision and the tenure range of that vision, and where you place your focus.

A mindset creates behaviors and thinking patterns. In her global bestseller Mindset: The Psychology of Success, psychologist Carol Dweck depicted a fixed mindset as one containing the beliefs that talent and abilities are innate, permanent, and resistant to effort. On the other hand, a belief that effort, learning from failure, and perseverance can improve performance was labeled by Dweck as a growth mindset.

Leaders with a fixed mindset end up demotivating their team members as their behaviors and thinking patterns end up breeding mistrust, stifling creativity, and creating a blame others culture. As a result, team members feel unappreciated by their leader and wind up with less commitment and higher disengagement. Naturally, the growth mindset enhances individual and team performance through encouragement, motivation, and turning errors into learning opportunities.

Big Five Leadership Mindset Traits

From my perspective, there are five critical values incumbent in a Great Leader Mindset: optimism, resiliency, confidence, humility, and gratitude. I call these the Big Five Great Leadership Mindset Traits. Let's look at each of these.

> **Optimism** — Optimism is known to boost energy levels, create higher levels of concentration and focus, improve the chances of reaching a set goal,

and prevent health problems from occurring. An optimistic leader will find, notice, and leverage the positives in any circumstance and in all challenges faced. This optimism must be based on reality (no rose-colored glasses here) and the honest belief that the leader and the team have the resources, talents, capabilities, and fortitude available to achieve success.

Resiliency — While some people just seem more naturally resilient, resiliency is a skill that can be learned, practiced, and improved over time. Resiliency is the ability to bounce back from adversity, misfortune, or change. It is also a spirit of hardiness and the strength (both physical and mental) to remain persistent in pursuit of a goal or in overcoming a challenge. A core component of resiliency is adaptability, which is built through becoming comfortable with ambiguity, taking control of our internal monologues, and paying particular attention to maintaining high levels of physical, mental, and emotional energy.

Confidence — Confidence is another component of a strong leadership mindset, provided it is held in check and not seen as self-promoting, ego-centric boosterism. Confidence in your skills and abilities will reduce stress and pressure, leading to better analysis, evaluation, and decision making. It comes from knowing yourself, and fully understanding (and appreciating) your strengths and weaknesses.

It also comes from observing and analyzing how you make decisions, both good and bad. Not every decision will work out as you expect. That's okay. The key is to reflect back on how and why you made a particular decision to learn about your decision-making capabilities and tendencies. This helps you grow as a leader and gives you greater confidence when you have to make judgment calls in areas where you may not be a technical subject matter expert.

Humility — Before writing his best-selling book *Good to Great,* Jim Collins and his team examined over 1400 companies to determine what distinguishes great companies from good ones. One of his findings was that exceptional leaders exhibit what might seem to be a conflicting blend of intense professional determination to achieve goals and objectives mixed with high levels of personal humility. These exceptional leaders displayed a constant ability to drive results by continuously recognizing the contributions of others rather than claiming all the credit or keeping the focus on themselves.

When a leader makes his or her team, or one of their employees, look good, it also makes the leader look good as well. Having a humble leadership mindset and giving credit to others enhances how a leader is perceived and evaluated by others, particularly in such key attributes as overall leadership effectiveness and capability, trustworthiness, and acting in sync with the organization's core values and principles.

Gratitude — Another key attribute that great leaders keep at the forefront of their leadership mindsets is gratitude. *"The combination of leadership and gratitude is extremely powerful,"* notes author Christine Comaford in an article in *Forbes* magazine. *"The power of gratitude gives leaders the edge they need to quickly pivot during stressful situations."* We will discuss the element of gratitude further in chapter 6 under the topic of leading employee engagement.

Developing Your Own Leadership Mindset

Much like having your own personal leadership philosophy (see the previous chapter), to become a great leader also requires the development of your own leadership mindset based on your own set of personal values and beliefs.

Some of the core values you may want to include in your personal leadership mindset philosophy could be: resilience, adaptability, keen focus on people development, having a vision grounded in reality, or even becoming more mindful and conscious of your decisions, actions, and behaviors

The important thing is that the values must be your own — things you deeply believe in and care about. They cannot just be a list of positive attributes that you find in a book or online.

No matter what attributes and values you choose, however, trust overrides them all. Without trust, none of your other attributes and values matter. Trust is something you earn and maintain through your behaviors. It is not bestowed upon you by rank or title.

Quotes on
Leadership Mindset

Any change, even a change for the better, is always accompanied by drawbacks and discomforts.
Arnold Bennett

It had long since come to my attention that people of accomplishment rarely sat back and let things happen to them. They went out and happened to things.
Leonardo Da Vinci

If you resist change, you will face challenges on a daily basis. If you consciously refocus your attitude to see the benefits of change, your outlook becomes positive and life becomes easier.
Catherine Pulsifer

You cannot consistently perform in a manner which is inconsistent with the way you see yourself.
Zig Ziglar

Optimism is the one quality more associated with success and happiness than any other.
Brian Tracy

We lead by being human. We do not lead by being corporate, professional or institutional.
Paul Hawken

During critical periods, a leader is not allowed to feel sorry for himself, to be down, to be angry, or to be weak. Leaders must beat back these emotions.
Mike Krzyzewski

The challenge of leadership is to be strong but not rude; be kind, but not weak; be bold, but not a bully; be humble, but not timid; be proud, but not arrogant; have humor, but without folly.
Jim Rohn

The one who asks questions doesn't lose his way.
African Proverb

Courage is what it takes to stand up and speak; courage is also what it takes to sit down and listen.
Winston Churchill

With courage you will dare to take risks, have the strength to be compassionate and the wisdom to be humble. Courage is the foundation of integrity.
Keshavan Nair

Chase your passion, not your pension!
Denis Waitley

Sincerity is the treasure of a land, for it is in sincerity that the people find their strength in times of hardship.
Confucius

The three "C's" of leadership are Consideration, Caring, and Courtesy. Be polite to everyone.
Brian Tracy

If you wish others to believe in you, you must first convince them that you believe in them.
Harvey Mackay

To be yourself in a world that is constantly trying to make you something else is the greatest accomplishment.
Ralph Waldo Emerson

You should never let your fears prevent you from doing what you know is right.
Aung San Suu Kyi

We gain strength, and courage, and confidence by each experience in which we really stop to look fear in the face. We must do that which we think we cannot.
Eleanor Roosevelt

The greatest enemy of knowledge is not ignorance, it is the illusion of knowledge.
Stephen Hawking

Your belief determines your action and your action determines your results, but first you have to believe.
Mark Victor Hansen

He can who thinks he can, and he can't who thinks he can't. This is an inexorable, indisputable law.
Henry Ford

The ability to perceive or think differently is more important than the knowledge gained.
David Bohm

Do you understand if you're going to lead, you're going to serve?
John Calipari

Keep your fears to yourself, but share your courage with others.
Robert Louis Stevenson

When everything seems to be going against you, remember that the airplane takes off against the wind, not with it.
Henry Ford

Leadership is not a right; it's a responsibility.
John Maxwell

Determination gives you the resolve to keep going in spite of the roadblocks that lay before you.
Denis Waitley

Optimism is essential to achievement and it is also the foundation of courage and true progress.
Nicholas Murray Butler

Shift your momentum, and a bad day turns into a great day. Problems change into opportunities. What was once negative energy turns into a useful, creative force.
Ralph Marston

Every problem has a gift for you in its hands.
Richard Bach

Never assume you understand. Ask the questions.
Brian Tracy

The act of being wise is knowing what to overlook.
William James

There is no passion to be found playing small, in settling for a life that is less than the one you are capable of living.
Nelson Mandela

Believe and act as if it were impossible to fail.
Charles F. Kettering

Your greatness does not need to be proven. Only exhibited.
Steven B. Howard

Strength is a matter of a made up mind.
John Beecher

Man is what he believes.
Anton Chekhov

You can do a thing only if you have the belief that it can be done.
Anonymous

If you don't stand for something, you will fall for anything.
Malcolm X

Keep your dreams alive. Understand to achieve anything requires faith and belief in yourself, vision, hard work, determination, and dedication. Remember all things are possible for those who believe.
Gail Devers

It's what you choose to believe that makes you the person you are.
Karen Marie Moning

In the province of the mind, what one believes to be true either is true or becomes true.
John Lilly

By nature we have no defect that could not become a strength, no strength that could not become a defect.
Johann Wolfgang von Goethe

Men willingly believe what they wish.
Julius Caesar

What we can or cannot do, what we consider possible or impossible, is rarely a function of our true capability. It is more likely a function of our beliefs about who we are.
Anthony Robbins

There is no limit to what you can imagine. And with commitment, with effort, what you can imagine you can become. Put your mind to work for you. Believe that you can do it. The world will tell you that you can't. Yet, in your belief you'll find the strength, you'll find the ability, to do it anyway.
Ralph Marston

He who has a WHY to live for can bear almost any HOW.
Friedrich Nietzsche

No one can defeat us unless we first defeat ourselves.
Dwight D. Eisenhower

A great attitude becomes a great mood, which becomes a great day, which becomes a great year, which becomes a great life.
Zig Ziglar

If it is once again one against forty-eight, then I am very sorry for the forty-eight.
Margaret Thatcher

The easiest thing to be in the world is you. The most difficult thing to be is what other people want you to be. Don't let them put you in that position.
Leo Buscaglia

Incredible change happens in your life when you decide to take control of what you do have power over instead of craving control over what you don't.
Steve Maraboli

The man who does not value himself, cannot value anything or anyone.
Ayn Rand

Who looks outside, dreams; who looks inside, awakens.
Carl Jung

If you have a strong mind and plant in it a firm resolve, you can change your destiny.
Paramahansa Yogananda

Make sure your worst enemy doesn't live between your own two ears.
Laird Hamilton

What positive things have you said to yourself today? Acknowledge your greatness.
Chalene Johnson

We need to accept that we won't always make the right decisions, that we'll screw up royally sometimes — understanding that failure is not the opposite of success; it's part of success.
Arianna Huffington

Leadership and learning are indispensable to each other.
John F. Kennedy

Having a positive attitude does not prevent you from having to face challenges. Positive thoughts, though, will help you cope with the challenges you face so you can take advantage of opportunities within them.
Byron Pulsifer

Begin challenging your own assumptions. Your assumptions are your windows on the world. Scrub them off every once and a while, or the light won't come in.
Alan Alda

Nurture your mind with great thoughts; to believe in the heroic makes heroes.
Benjamin Disraeli

The pessimist sees difficulty in every opportunity. The optimist sees opportunity in every difficulty.
Winston Churchill

Most people believe their beliefs have been defined by their reality. Instead, their reality has been defined by their beliefs.
Mike Dooley

Our deepest fear is not that we are inadequate. Our deepest fear is that we are powerful beyond measure.
Marianne Williamson

Know thyself.
Temple of Apollo

Do or do not. There is no try.
Yoda

The problem is not the problem. The problem is your attitude about the problem.
Captain Jack Sparrow

It's what you learn after you know it all that counts.
John Wooden

Never stop learning because life never stops teaching.
Steven B. Howard

To be successful you must accept all challenges that come your way. You can't just accept the ones you like.
Mike Gafka

It's not about the shoes. It's about what you do in them.
Michael Jordan

A positive attitude causes a chain reaction of positive thoughts, events, and outcomes. It is a catalyst, and it sparks extraordinary results.
Wade Boggs

Leadership is a mindset that shifts from being a victim to creating results. Any one of us can demonstrate leadership in our work and within our lives.
Robin S. Sharma

Be a yardstick of quality. Some people aren't used to an environment where excellence is expected.
Steve Jobs

The question isn't who's going to let me; it's who is going to stop me.
Ayn Rand

Man often becomes what he believes himself to be. If I keep on saying to myself that I cannot do a certain thing, it is possible that I may end by really becoming incapable of doing it. On the contrary, if I shall have the belief that I can do it, I shall surely acquire the capacity to do it, even if I may not have it at the beginning.
Mohandas Karamchand (Mahatma) Gandhi

The most common way people give up their power is by thinking they don't have any.
Alice Walker

Never argue with an idiot. They drag you down to their level then beat you with experience.
Dilbert

Throw yourself into some work you believe in with all your heart, live for it, die for it, and you will find the happiness that you had thought could never be yours.
Dale Carnegie

Your work is to discover your work and then with all your heart to give yourself to it.
Buddha

If you spend too much time thinking about a thing, you'll never get it done. Make at least one definite move daily towards your goal.
Bruce Lee

Having a positive mental attitude is asking how something can be done rather than saying it can't be done.
Bo Bennett

When it's tough, will you give up, or will you be relentless?
Jeff Bezos

When you think everything is someone else's fault, you will suffer a lot. When you realize that everything springs only from yourself, you will learn both peace and joy.
Dalai Lama

The best of us are those who help the rest of us.
Anthony Douglas Williams

CHAPTER 4

Leading Teams and People

G reat leaders know that sustainable, repeatable, replicable success results from collaborative, collective, and engaged efforts. This is why great leaders concentrate on the people side of success, including motivation, team building, the interpersonal skills of team members, group recognition, and group rewards.

When it comes to leading people, leaders have four distinct audiences:

> The teams that report to them.
>
> Cross-functional teams that they lead.
>
> Individuals who directly report to them.
>
> Individuals, peers, and colleagues with whom they work.

For each of these audiences, a different set of leadership skills and approaches is required. However, there is one common factor — since they are dealing with individuals, or a collection of individuals, each people leadership situation requires an individualized approach suited for the various demeanors, motivational needs, and communication preferences of those being led.

This means that great leaders must be flexible in their leadership approach and with the motivational and communication tactics they use.

Leading Teams

Leading teams is fraught with peril and numerous opportunities for mistakes, especially by new or inexperienced leaders. This is mostly due to the dynamic nature of teams, including how the individuals on a team interact with one another.

The two team leadership concepts I have found most useful are *The Nature of Teams* by Dr. Bruce Tuckman and *The Five Dysfunctions of Teams* by Patrick Lencioni

You can easily find good information on both of these team leadership models on the Internet.

Not all groups of individuals comprise a true team. Even when managers talk about "my team" often this is really only a group of individuals performing similar, but not necessarily inter-related work, who all happen to report to the same individual.

As I have often said in my leadership development programs: *"A team is not a group of people who work together. A team is a group of people working together towards a shared outcome who trust and respect each other."*

Preventing team dysfunction is a primary concern of a great leader. This often requires an unbiased assessment of individual actions and motives, as well as keen eyes and ears for the early warning signals shown in Lencioni's The Five Dysfunctions of a Team model.

Trust and respect among team members, and between the team leader and team members, is critical. Relationships and trust between team members far outweigh immediate results. After all, if the trust is gone, future collaboration and working partnerships will simply not happen.

Great leaders excel at creating and maintaining high-performing cohesive teams, which are characterized by:

>Utilization of the diverse skills, knowledge, and experience of all team members.

Alignment around mutually agreed upon common objectives and goals.

Robust conversations and debates on critical issues that lead to high-quality decisions.

Individual and group accountability.

Learning from mistakes.

Fixing problems by looking for solutions, not blame.

Communicating As A Leader

Communicating is at the heart of leadership. Almost by definition great leaders are great communicators. In fact, I cannot think of any great leaders who were poor communicators.

For many years being great at leadership communication was thought to be a function of using the right words, exhibiting the right passions, and delivering one's message in a strong, forceful manner. And while that approach worked pretty well in the old command and control generation of leadership, there is a whole lot more today to being a great communicator.

If your internal communication is not good, and by that I mean clear and concise, then your external communication (either outside your department or outside your organization) will likely end up being centered on rationalizing and explaining negative outcomes and events. A leader cannot be muddled and disorganized when communicating within his or her organization and expect to be a clear and focused communicator outside it.

Leaders must take time to clearly communicate with their teams and team members. And this starts with being equally good at two critical communication skills: questioning and listening.

Questioning Skills

Great leaders ask the right kinds of questions in order to get to the root causes of a problem or to determine the full scope of a team member's concerns or issues.

They also ask the right questions to ensure that they are getting complete details and the full story of a situation. Great leaders know that too often subordinates are inclined to say what they think the leader wants to hear rather than their own assessment and knowledge of a situation.

Even when all the right questions have been asked and answered, great leaders do their own checking of facts, data, and missing information.

Listening Skills

To start with, great communicators are great listeners. And so are great leaders. In fact, I always tell my leadership development participants that since they each have two ears and one mouth, they should use these proportionately in communicating as a leader. In other words, they will benefit most from listening twice as much as they speak.

I firmly believe that listening is the number one communication skill a leader must have. This is particularly true for new leaders, as the tendency is to think that once one is put into a leadership position it is a requirement to have all the answers and to bark out all the orders. Nothing could be further from the truth.

There is more to listening than simply hearing the words others are saying. Rather, leaders need to develop their active listening skills, which means observing the emotions, feelings, expressions, and body language behind what is being said. It also means acutely listening for what is not being said and for what is intentionally being left out.

Stephen Covey, author of the book *The 7 Habits of Highly Effective People*, identified a key problem in communicating, both professionally and personally. He noted that too many of us *"listen with the intent to respond, not with the intent to understand."*

Listening with the intent to understand is a crucial skill for leaders. Fortunately, it is also one that can be developed and enhanced through practice and reflection.

All of these communication techniques, when used repeatedly in your daily communications with team members, will make you a better leader.

Quotes on Leading People and Teams

You manage things; you lead people.
Rear Admiral Grace Murray Hopper

Leaders must be close enough to relate to others, but far enough ahead to motivate them.
John Maxwell

Give whatever you are doing and whoever you are with the gift of your attention.
Jim Rohn

Never tell people how to do things. Tell them what to do and they will surprise you with their ingenuity.
George S. Patton

A leader...is like a shepherd. He stays behind the flock, letting the most nimble go out ahead, whereupon the others follow, not realizing that all along they are being directed from behind.
Nelson Mandela

It is absolutely necessary for me to have persons that can think for me, as well as execute orders.
George Washington

A leader's role is to raise people's aspirations for what they can become and to release their energies so they will try to get there.
David Gergen

I love to surround myself with people who have heart and conscience.
Howard Schultz

The measure of success is not just how many hands are working, but how well they are working together.
Ron Kaufman

The Law of Win/Win says: Let's not do it your way or my way; let's do it the best way.
Greg Anderson

I haven't always recruited for the best talent. I've taken a few guys who would fit for different reasons — leadership, toughness.
Tom Izzo

Power isn't control at all — power is strength, and giving that strength to others. A leader isn't someone who forces others to make him stronger; a leader is someone willing to give his strength to others that they may have the strength to stand on their own.
Beth Revis

A leader takes people where they want to go. A great leader takes people where they don't necessarily want to go, but ought to be.
Rosalynn Carter

Remember, teamwork begins by building trust. And the only way to do that is to overcome our need for invulnerability.
Patrick Lencioni

Average leaders raise the bar on themselves; good leaders raise the bar for others; great leaders inspire others to raise their own bar.
Orrin Woodward

A good leader leads the people from above them. A great leader leads the people from within them.
M. D. Arnold

A great person attracts great people and knows how to hold them together.
Johann Wolfgang von Goethe

One person with a belief is equal to a force of ninety-nine with only interests.
John Stuart Mills

The man who gets the most satisfactory results is not always the man with the most brilliant single mind, but rather the man who can best coordinate the brains and talents of his associates.
Sir William Alton Jones

The quality of an organization can never exceed the quality of the minds that make it up.
Harold R. McAlindon

Nothing is more despicable than respect based on fear.
Albert Camus

Truth dies but mistrust blossoms.
Sophocles

If you don't realize there is always somebody who knows how to do something better than you, then you don't give proper respect for others' talents.
Hortense Canady

Kind words are short and easy to speak, but their echoes are truly endless.
Mother Teresa

It's not what you tell them, it's what they hear that matters.
Red Auerbach

Perhaps you will forget tomorrow the kind words you say today, but the recipient may cherish them over a lifetime.
Dale Carnegie

You will regret many things in life but you will never regret being too kind or too fair.
Brian Tracy

It costs you nothing to be lavish with your praise.
Ron Kaufman

Wise men are not always silent, but they know when to be.
Anonymous

There are two ways of exerting one's strength: one is pushing down, the other is pulling up.
Booker T. Washington

You start to realize that the trophy brings you nothing of real value. Nothing, really. The joy in coaching is helping a group of kids accomplish something they couldn't accomplish by themselves.
Billy Donovan

Always to try to be a little kinder than is necessary.
James M. Barrie

Tell a man he is brave, and you help him to become so.
Thomas Carlyle

People are basically good; if you give them the right tools they'll prove it to you every day.
Charlie Rose

Kind words do not cost much. Yet they accomplish much.
Blaise Pascal

No one who achieves success does so without the help of others. The wise and confident acknowledge this help with gratitude.
Alfred North Whitehead

Keep your eyes open and try to catch people in your company doing something right, then praise them for it.
Tom Hopkins

Tend to the people, and they will tend to the business.
John Maxwell

People often say that motivation doesn't last. Well, neither does bathing — that's why we recommend it daily.
Zig Ziglar

The secret of discipline is motivation. When a man is sufficiently motivated, discipline will take care of itself.
Sir Alexander Paterson

The single common denominator of men and women who achieve great things is a sense of destiny.
Brian Tracy

A decision is made with the brain. A commitment is made with the heart. Therefore, a commitment is much deeper and more binding than a decision.
Nido Qubein

While you can be efficient with things, you can't be efficient effectively with people.
Stephen Covey

The difference between a successful person and others is not a lack of strength, not a lack of knowledge, but rather a lack in will.
Vince Lombardi

Spirit has fifty times the strength and staying power of brawn and muscle.
Mark Twain

Be quick to praise people.
Bernard Baruch

All human actions have one or more of these seven causes: chance, nature, compulsions, habit, reason, passion, desire.
Aristotle

A team is not a group of people who work together. A team is a group of people working together towards a shared outcome who trust and respect each other.
Steven B. Howard

What is a committee? A group of the unwilling, picked from the unfit, to do the unnecessary.
Richard Harkness

When someone does something good, applaud! You will make two people happy.
Samuel Goldwyn

The most difficult thing for individuals to do when they're part of the team is to sacrifice. Without sacrifice you'll never know your team's potential.
Pat Riley

There is little difference in people, but that little difference makes a big difference. The little difference is attitude. The big difference is whether it is positive or negative.
W. Clement Stone

Individuals with great self-esteem will do great things...they're the ones others count on to boost results when the company needs it most.
Rick Pitino

My staff is a complementary team of independent thinkers.
Leroy Jethro Gibbs

Conflict is the gadfly of thought. It stirs us to observation and memory. It instigates us to invention. It shocks us out of sheep-like passivity, and sets us at noting and contriving, reflection and ingenuity.
John Dewey

Conflict is inevitable, but combat is optional.
Max Lucado

The aim of an argument or discussion should not be victory, but progress.
Joseph Joubert

If everyone is thinking alike then somebody isn't thinking.
George S. Patton

Direct confrontation, direct conversation is real respect.
Penn Jillette

Honest disagreement is often a good sign of progress.
Mohandas Karamchand (Mahatma) Gandhi

By harnessing your imagination you can focus on problems and opportunities in ways that lead to value-adding innovations. Those organizations which encourage employees to contribute ideas will always do better than those that do not. The reason is simple. Innovative organizations can still fail, as can innovative ideas. But innovative organizations will maximize their opportunities and find more creative solutions to their problems.
Ed Bernacki

One man practicing sportsmanship is far better than a hundred teaching it.
Knute Rockne

Trust men and they will be true to you; treat them greatly and they will show themselves great.
Ralph Waldo Emerson

You may be deceived if you trust too much, but you will live in torment if you don't trust enough.
Frank Crane

One must be fond of people and trust them if one is not to make a mess of life.
E. M. Forster

Whatever words we utter should be chosen with care for people will hear them and be influenced by them for good or ill.
Buddha

The organization that can't communicate can't change, and the corporation that can't change is dead.
Nido Qubein

The 8 key words that will move practically anyone to your side of the issue: If you can't do it, I'll definitely understand.
Bob Burg

Poor or fuzzy communications are major time-wasters. Take the time to be crystal-clear in your communications with others.
Brian Tracy

The most important thing in communication is to hear what isn't being said.
Peter Drucker

The goal of effective communication should be for listeners to say, "me, too!" versus "So what?"
Jim Rohn

Actions speak louder than words.
English Proverb

Words are potent weapons for all causes, good or bad.
Manly P. Hall

A person hears only what they understand.
Johann Wolfgang von Goethe

Speak honestly or else be silent.
Rumi

Seek first to understand, then to be understood.
Stephen Covey

Skill in the art of communication is crucial to a leader's success. You can accomplish nothing unless you communicate effectively.
Norman Allen

To effectively communicate, we must realize that we are all different in the way we perceive the world and use this understanding as a guide to our communication with others.
Anthony Robbins

To be persuasive, we must be believable; to be believable, we must be credible; to be credible, we must be truthful.
Edward R. Murrow

Communication does not always occur naturally, even among a tight-knit group of individuals. Communication must be taught and practiced in order to bring everyone together as one.
Mike Krzyzewski

A speech should not just be a sharing of information, but a sharing of yourself.
Ralph Archbold

Storytellers, by the very act of telling, communicate a radical learning that changes lives and the world: telling stories is a universally accessible means through which people make meaning.
Chris Cavanaugh

Good communication is as stimulating as black coffee, and just as hard to sleep after.
Anne Morrow Lindbergh

Most successful people I've known are the ones who do more listening than talking.
Bernard Baruch

Two monologues do not make a dialogue.
Jeff Daly

The right word may be effective, but no word was ever as effective as a rightly timed pause.
Samuel Langhorne Clemens (Mark Twain)

Leaders who do not listen will eventually be surrounded by people who refuse to speak.
Steven B. Howard

The way to get things done is not to mind who gets the credit for doing them.
Benjamin Jowett

Treat people as if they were what they ought to be and you will help them become what they are capable of becoming.
Johann Wolfgang von Goethe

The human spirit, like a fire, must be lit again each day.
Steve Chandler

I praise loudly; I blame softly.
Catherine the Second

Nothing lowers the level of conversation more than raising the voice.
Stanley Horowitz

Human beings don't engage by being managed.
Daniel Pink

Leadership is all about people. It is not about organizations. It is not about plans. It is not about strategies. It is all about people-motivating people to get the job done. You have to be people-centered.
Colin Powell

The most important thing is to try and inspire people so that they can be great in whatever they want to do.
Kobe Bryant

It's a very funny thing about life; if you refuse to accept anything but the best, you very often get it.
William Somerset Maugham

The fact is that people are good. Give people affection and security, and they will give affection and be secure in their feelings and their behavior.
Abraham Maslow

Don't waste talent. No matter what you do, don't waste talent.
Ray Lewis

No act of kindness, no matter how small, is ever wasted.
Aesop

Not the cry but the flight of the wild duck leads the flock to fly and follow.
Chinese Proverb

Everybody counts, everybody deserves a chance, everybody has a responsible role to play and we all do better when we work together.
Bill Clinton

Most businesses think that product is the most important thing, but without great leadership, mission and a team that delivers results at a high level, even the best product won't make a company successful.
Robert Kiyosaki

The leaders who work most effectively, it seems to me, never say "I." And that's not because they have trained themselves not to say "I." They don't think I. They think "we"; they think "team."' They understand their job to be to make the team function. They accept responsibility and don't sidestep it, but "we" gets the credit. This is what creates trust, what enables you to get the task done.
Peter Drucker

People are like stained-glass windows. They sparkle and shine when the sun is out, but when the darkness sets in their true beauty is revealed only if there is light from within.
Elisabeth Kübler-Ross

The true measure of team leadership is not about how many team members are working, but how well they are working together.
Steven B. Howard

The achievements of an organization are the results of the combined effort of each individual.
Vince Lombardi

To win in the marketplace, you must first win in the workplace.
Doug Conant

Genius is there in all of us, just waiting for us to tap into it.
Robert R. Toth

Accept the fact that we have to treat almost anybody as a volunteer.
Peter Drucker

Always treat your employees exactly as you want them to treat your best customers.
Stephen Covey

Employees who believe that management is concerned about them as a whole person — not just an employee — are more productive, more satisfied, more fulfilled Satisfied employees mean satisfied customers, which leads to profitability.
Anne M. Mulcahy

Leaders who don't listen will eventually be surrounded by people unwilling to speak and contribute.
Steven B. Howard

Fairness is not an attitude. It's a professional skill that must be developed and exercised.
Brit Hume

Business and human endeavors are systems. We tend to focus on snapshots of isolated parts of the system. And wonder why our deepest problems never get solved.
Peter Senge

Three things in human life are important: the first is to be kind; the second is to be kind; and the third is to be kind.
Henry James

The gem cannot be polished without friction, nor man perfected without trials.
Chinese Proverb

The influence of each human being on others in this life is a kind of immortality.
John Quincy Adams

Speaking your mind is an awfully dangerous thing to do. Choose your words carefully.
Rick Beneteau

A good objective of leadership is to help those who are doing poorly to do well and to help those who are doing well to do even better.
Jim Rohn

Be quick to praise people.
Bernard Baruch

My father gave me the greatest gift anyone could give another person: He believed in me.
Jim Valvano

Tenderness and kindness are not signs of weakness and despair but manifestations of strength and resolution.
Kahlil Gibran

If we could look into each other's hearts, and understand the unique challenges each of us faces, I think we would treat each other more gently, with more love, patience, tolerance, and care.
Marvin J. Ashton

When dealing with people, remember you are not dealing with creatures of logic, but creatures of emotion.
Dale Carnegie

Honest disagreement is often a good sign of progress.
Mohandas Karamchand (Mahatma) Gandhi

It is never wise to appear to be more clever than you are. It is sometimes wise to appear slightly less so.
William Whitelaw

Basketball is a team game but that doesn't mean all five players should have the same amount of shots.
Dean Smith

Surround yourself with the best people you can find, delegate authority, and don't interfere as long as the policy you've decided upon is being carried out.
Ronald Reagan

A great person attracts great people and knows how to hold them together.
Johann Wolfgang von Goethe

I think perfect objectivity is an unrealistic goal; fairness, however, is not.
Michael Pollan

If you hire only those people you understand, the company will never get people better than you are. Always remember that you often find outstanding people among those you don't particularly like.
Soichiro Honda

Never ruin an apology with an excuse.
Kimberly Howard

Talent wins games, but teamwork and intelligence wins championships.
Michael Jordan

The main ingredient of stardom is the rest of the team.
John Wooden

Genuine sincerity opens people's hearts, while manipulation causes them to close.
Daisaku Ikeda

Tell me a fact and I'll learn. Tell me a truth and I'll believe. But tell me a story and it will live in my heart forever.
Native American Indian Proverb

The best executive is the one who has sense enough to pick good men to do what he wants done, and self-restraint to keep from meddling with them while they do it.
Theodore Roosevelt

You don't lead by pointing and telling people some place to go. You lead by going to that place and making a case.
Ken Kesey

You can't live a perfect day without doing something for someone who will never be able to repay you.
John Wooden

Remember there's no such thing as a small act of kindness. Every act creates a ripple with no logical end.
Scott Adams

I think one of the keys to leadership is recognizing that everybody has gifts and talents. A good leader will learn how to harness those gifts toward the same goal.
Ben Carson

I put my talents on the shoulders of someone else's talent.
Michael Jordan

Unhappiness is best defined as the difference between our talents and our expectations.
Edward de Bono

You can work as an individual, but you'll win with a team.
Ron Kaufman

The key to motivation is motive.
Stephen Covey

CHAPTER 5

Leading People Development

The people development aspect of leadership is often overlooked by leaders, especially by those put into leadership positions for the first time, such as new supervisors, frontline managers, and newly appointed sales managers who have been promoted due to high sales performance.

Leaders whose key aim is to attract followers are interested in authority, power, status, and control. They drive to make people get things done — usually their way (or the highway). While this often produces wonderful short-term results, it is not a sustainable or replicable leadership methodology. It also tends to lead to employee burnout and high employee attrition rates.

However, all great leaders know that their mission is not to create followers, but to create more good leaders for their organizations. This is why people development is a core component of the art of great leadership.

Here is a revealing exercise that I run in my leadership development programs and one-on-one coaching sessions. If you would like to participate, grab a writing instrument and a piece of paper.

The exercise is to answer these three questions while thinking about a typical two-week period at work:

1) What percentage of your time is spent attending meetings, participating in conference calls, or reading/responding/deleting/sending emails?

2) What percentage of your time is spent reviewing work progress or results (this includes reading and reviewing documents or reports), or on generating reports or presentations related to work progress or results?

3) What percentage of your time is spent doing Individual Contributor work?

Add up the three figures. Is the total higher than 80%? Higher than 90%?

Subtract the total from 100. That's the percent of time remaining in your typical work life for developing your people.

For many leaders, especially mid-level leaders and supervisors, people development time is less than 15%. Yet people development is (or should be) one of the key priorities for all leaders, as it is one of the most important drivers of sustainable success for any organization.

In fact, I would suggest that people development should be the single most important priority for all leaders. After all, if a leader is one who achieves progress through the involvement and actions of others, then greater progress will be made when the people being led are constantly being developed and improved.

Additionally, great leaders know that people development can be a highly leveraged catalyst for individuals as well as for the organization. That is why the best leadership talent is bringing out the talent in others.

Developing People and Teams

Not surprisingly, the 2017 FORTUNE 100 Best Companies to Work For annual study showed that the best companies are committed to employee development. In fact, the companies on this list devote an average of 65 hours per annum toward developing salaried employees. They also invest an average of 58 hours per year for the development of their hourly workers.

A focus on people development differentiates the best companies to work for from all others. A focus on people development is also one of the actions that differentiates great leaders from good leaders.

Everyone on your team has talents that can be improved. These can be the functional skills needed to perform their jobs, or the interpersonal skills required to get work done in collaboration or cooperation with others. Great leaders ensure that all members of their teams receive on-going development, both formally and informally.

This is nothing new. For, as John Quincy Adams noted centuries ago, *"If your actions inspire others to dream more, learn more, do more, and become more, you are a leader."* Unfortunately, however, a focus by leaders on developing the skills of their people has been misplaced in recent decades by an overemphasis on quarterly profits and other short-term performance measurements.

So how do you go about being an excellent leader of people development?

First, have an understanding that developing the skills of your team members is your responsibility as a leader. Your organization's Human Resources and Talent Development departments are resources for you to use in this endeavor. But it is your responsibility to ensure the continuous development of your team members and yourself, not theirs.

Speaking of which, it is also important to understand that your own continuous development as a leader is also your responsibility (as well as your boss's). We will delve into the subject of your own personal leadership development in chapter ten.

There are so many resources, both free and paid, on leadership and skill development available through the Internet (articles, videos, book excerpts, workshops, and learning programs) that

Steven B. Howard

there is no valid excuse for any leader to not be constantly upgrading their leadership, motivational, communication, collaboration, coaching, and people development skills. I have a list of highly recommended leadership resources on our company website at www.CalienteLeadership.com.

Tools for People Development

There are six main methodologies for leading people development, including three that come under the traditional heading of training. These six methods are:

1) Feedback

2) Coaching

3) Delegation

4) On-the-job training

5) Team training

6) Formal classroom training

The 70-20-10 Model for Learning and Development states that individuals obtain 70% of their work-related knowledge from job-related experiences, 20% from interactions with others, and 10% from formal education events such as training programs.

Hence, as a leader of people, you should focus your team member development efforts, for both teams and individuals, on the first five methods above. Your Human Resources and Talent Development colleagues should take the lead only on formal training events, which include both classroom and virtual training programs.

Feedback is a specialized form of professional development, one with which many new managers and leaders struggle. Part of the reason for this is that feedback has been taught as either positive or negative, with the latter difficult to deliver.

To make the delivery of negative feedback easier, managers and leaders have for years been taught the "sandwich model," in which negative feedback is sandwiched between so-called positive feedback statements.

This process really does not work. As soon as you give someone a piece of positive feedback, they wait for the "but…" to appear. Telling someone they have "done something well, but…" negates the positive impact of the opening words.

When giving feedback your intention should be to help someone build competency and/or confidence in their abilities by helping them determine how to change or improve performance. Basically, your intention when giving feedback should be to help someone learn and develop.

Hence, if your intention is to help someone improve, learn, or develop how could any feedback be perceived as negative? All leaders should dump the phrases "positive feedback" and "negative feedback" from their terminology. Instead, replace these with the phrases "reinforcing feedback" and "developmental feedback."

Use reinforcing feedback when you want to reinforce performance or behavior that is producing desired results and outcomes. Your goal here is recognition of what a person is doing well in order to encourage and motivate them to continue doing so more frequently or in other relevant situations. This not only improves the likelihood of such performance or behavior being repeated, it also builds confidence in the person receiving such feedback.

Use developmental feedback when there is a need to provide corrective instructions or to help someone determine how to change or improve their performance. Again, it is given with the intention of helping that person learn and develop, as well as shaping desired behavior and increasing the likelihood that future performance will be improved.

Providing feedback is also a factor in increasing employee engagement, but only if it is done in the proper way. A leader's intention in giving feedback to a team member must always be for the purpose of helping the employee improve performance or behavior. Feedback should never be given when upset, angered, or disappointed with a direct report or colleague.

Additionally, the purpose of feedback should never be to belittle or disparage the employee, make them feel less-than-adequate, or with the intention of punishing the team member. And, of course, scolding an employee is neither a form of coaching nor proper engagement-inducing feedback.

This is not to say there is no place for corrective feedback in the workplace. Part of personal development means learning from mistakes and errors. If someone is doing something wrong, then corrective feedback is mandatory. But it will only be engagement-inducing and productive feedback if such corrective feedback is given *with the intention* of helping the other person improve performance or behavior. Thus, leaders need to offer feedback that helps and inspires team members to perform at higher, more productive levels, not cut them down to size through criticism, ridicule, or denigrating remarks.

All feedback should be delivered in an on-going, timely and non-judgmental manner. It also needs to be specific, descriptive, detailed, actionable, and future-focused. You are not looking for ownership of blame here or excuses. You are looking for ways to improve future performance or to correct unacceptable behavior going forward.

Quotes on Leading People Development

What you leave behind is not what is engraved in stone monuments, but what is woven into the lives of others.
Pericles

Before you become a leader, success is all about growing yourself. When you become a leader success is all about growing others.
Jack Welch

It is the nature of man to rise to greatness if greatness is expected of him.
John Steinbeck

The nobler sort of man emphasizes the good qualities in others, and does not accentuate the bad. The inferior does the reverse.
Confucius

Helping those who have lost their way is felt across the universe.
Anthony Douglas Williams

I hear and I forget.
I see and I remember.
I do and I understand.
Confucius

Praise, like gold and diamonds, owes its value only to its scarcity.
Samuel Johnson

Giving connects two people, the giver and the receiver, and this connection gives birth to a new sense of belonging.
Deepak Chopra

Deal with the faults of others as gently as with your own.
Chinese Proverb

Think twice before you speak, because your words and influence will plant the seed of either success or failure in the mind of another.
Napoleon Hill

Each of us sooner or later realizes that our relationships with others require giving of ourselves — not only of our time, but our sincere and caring involvement as well. Too often we close the book on the many who need us by allotting just so much of ourselves, and end by being miserly with what should be the easiest and least expensive thing to give — ourselves.
Leo Buscaglia

A great mentor is one who aims for others' abilities to surpass his own.
Anonymous

Practice does not make perfect; perfect practice makes perfect.
Vince Lombardi

Giving whether it be of time, labor, affection, advice, gifts, or whatever, is one of life's greatest pleasures.
Rebecca Russell

Flatter me, and I may not believe you. Criticize me, and I may not like you. Ignore me, and I may not forgive you. Encourage me, and I may not forget you.
William Arthur

Instead of always harping on a man's faults, tell him of his virtues. Try to pull him out of his rut of bad habits. Hold up to him his better self, his real self that can dare and do and win out.
Eleanor H. Porter

Outstanding leaders go out of their way to boost the self-esteem of their personnel. If people believe in themselves, it's amazing what they can accomplish.
Sam Walton

Gentle words, quiet words, are after all the most powerful words. They are more convincing, compelling and prevailing.
Washington Gladden

Part of coaching is acting. It's true of any kind of leadership, whether you're a CEO, an army general, or a father. Part of the job is that you don't reveal your own apprehensions.
John Calipari

We all need people who will give us feedback. That's how we improve.
Bill Gates

A lot of people have gone further than they thought they could because someone else thought they could.
Zig Ziglar

We often tend to build walls between work, family, and personal time. We act as if what we do in one area doesn't affect what we do in the others. Yet, we all know that these barriers are artificial.
Stephen Covey

You cannot succeed by yourself. It's hard to find a rich hermit.
Jim Rohn

The best way to add value to yourself is by adding value to other people.
John Maxwell

If I accept you as you are, I will make you worse; however, if I treat you as though you are what you are capable of becoming, I help you become that.
Johann Wolfgang von Goethe

The best of us are those who help the rest of us.
Anthony Douglas Williams

It is a fine thing to have ability, but the ability to discover ability in others is the true test.
Elbert Hubbard

Oversharpen the blade, and the edge will soon blunt.
Lao-Tzu

Everyone has huge creative capacities as a natural result of being a human being. The challenge is to develop them. A culture of creativity has to involve everybody not just a select few.
Sir Ken Robinson

Someone who is exceptional in their role is not just a little better than someone who is pretty good, they are 100 times better.
Mark Zuckerberg

People are your most valuable asset. Only people can be made to appreciate in value.
Stephen Covey

Continuous training of your employees, especially in the "soft skills" areas of teamwork, collaboration and working across boundaries, is the key to scaling every part of your business.
Steven B. Howard

Too many people overvalue what they are not and undervalue what they are.
Malcolm Forbes

The way to develop the best that is in a person is by appreciation and encouragement.
Charles Schwab

At times, our own light goes out and is rekindled by a spark from another person. Each of us has cause to think with deep gratitude of those who have lighted the flame within us.
Albert Schweitzer

My job is not to be easy on people. My job is to take these great people we have and to push them and make them even better.
Steve Jobs

All progress takes place outside the comfort zone.
Michael John Bobak

The greatest good you can do for another is to not just share your riches, but reveal to them their own.
Benjamin Disraeli

Judgments prevent us from seeing the good that lies beyond appearances.
Wayne Dyer

Adversity has the effect of eliciting talents which, in prosperous circumstances, would have lain dormant.
Horace

The most precious gift we can offer others is our presence. When mindfulness embraces those we love, they will bloom like flowers.
Thich Nhat Hanh

Motivation alone is not enough. If you have an idiot and you motivate them, now you have a motivated idiot.
Jim Rohn

The mediocre teacher tells. The good teacher explains. The superior teacher demonstrates. The great teacher inspires.
William Arthur Ward

Don't be stingy with your encouragement. Your words can be a catalyst for untold change in the lives of others.
Josh Hinds

The growth and development of people is the highest calling of leadership.
Harvey S. Firestone

If you have knowledge, let others light their candles in it.
Margaret Fuller

If you treat an individual as he is, he will remain how he is. But if you treat him as if he were what he ought to be and could be, he will become what he ought to be and could be.
Johann Wolfgang von Goethe

Perfection is not attainable, but if we chase perfection, we can catch excellence.
Vince Lombardi

A teacher affects eternity; he can never tell where his influence stops.
Henry Adams

One of the greatest gifts a leader can give to team members is to help them find their talents.
Steven B. Howard

Passion is the driver of achievement in all fields. Some people love doing things they don't feel they're good at. That may be because they underestimate their talents or haven't yet put the work in to develop them.
Sir Ken Robinson

My main job was developing talent. I was a gardener providing water and other nourishment to our top 750 people. Of course, I had to pull out some weeds, too.
Jack Welch

Survival of the fittest is not the same as survival of the best. Leaving leadership development up to chance is foolish.
Morgan McCall

Growing other leaders from the ranks isn't just the duty of leaders, it's an obligation.
Warren Bennis

Winning companies win because they have good leaders who nurture the development of other leaders at all levels of the organization.
Noel Tichy

Failing forward is the ability to get back up after you've been knocked down, learn from your mistake, and move forward in a better direction.
John Maxwell

I'll bet most of the companies that are in life-or-death battles got into that kind of trouble because they didn't pay enough attention to developing their leaders.
Wayne Calloway

Never try to teach a pig to sing; it wastes your time and it annoys the pig.
Paul Dickson

Learning is like rowing upstream; not to advance is to drop back.
Chinese Proverb

Developing talent is business's most important task—the sine qua non of competition in a knowledge economy.
Peter Drucker

I view my primary job as strengthening our talent pools. So I view every conversation, every meeting as an opportunity to talk about our talented people.
Jack Welch

There is no way to spend too much time on obtaining and developing the best people.
Larry Bossidy

Quality is one capability that GE has focused on for over a decade; talent management has been a focus for over fifty years.
Edward Lawler

Talented people are vital to our continued success, and we continuously invest in our associates, giving them the tools and training to succeed.
Indra Nooyi

Managers and the top leaders of the organization need to create an environment that is professional and motivational for top talent management and development since leadership capabilities become more important as a company becomes more global.
Erin Lap

A company that can leverage resources and management talents across a broad array of opportunities may have an efficiency advantage over firms that cannot.

Gary Hamel

Indeed, if other organizations are managing their staffing processes exclusively in terms of headcount and cost, more sophisticated organizations may well emerge as the victors in the more subtle game of talent management.

Wayne Cascio

One lesson is that it cannot be HR's talent management strategy. It has to be the way the company is being managed by all line managers and people managers.

Marcia Avedon

HR's role should be to provide expertise on how to manage human capital and to help with the implementation and design of the talent management programs of the organization.

Edward Lawler

I find that when something that should be happening isn't happening regarding talent management, even though the resources are available to make it happen, one of two reasons is the cause: lack of skill or lack of will.

Kimberly Janson

At Google, we front-load our people investment. This means the majority of our time and money spent on people is invested in attracting, assessing, and cultivating new hires.

Laszlo Bock

HR professionals can coach business leaders to raise employee and organizational productivity by setting standards, giving feedback, and becoming personal leadership trainers.
Dave Ulrich

Finding ways to retain employees long enough to reap the benefits of your investment is an important part of a talent management strategy.
Mirian Graddick

Talent management deserves as much focus as financial capital management in corporations.
Jack Welch

The degree to which there is a talent mindset that is broadly held in management is one of the key determinants of what makes talent management successful.
Marcia Avedon

CHAPTER 6

Leading Employee Engagement

After leading team member development, employee engagement is the number one role of every leader. The more engaged your team members the higher your results will be.

Most managers and leaders think that leading people is only about attaining desired performance results and helping people cope with, accept, and implement change.

I would argue that great leaders accomplish great results and implement change by focusing on employee engagement. Great leaders know that performance results and change implementation are actually best derived from the engagement and motivation of team members.

Unfortunately, employee engagement remains stubbornly stagnant at unacceptably low levels.

In late 2013, the Deloitte Center for the Edge surveyed approximately 3000 workers in the U.S. across 15 industries. The results showed that almost 88% of those surveyed do not contribute to their full potential in their jobs because they do not have passion for their work. That leaves just 12% of the U.S. workforce possessing what Deloitte calls "the attributes of worker passion."

Employee engagement should be a critical concern of all leaders today, but apparently it is not. I say this because Gallup has been monitoring employee engagement around the world for years, and the needle hardly ever moves. Either few leaders are taking employee disengagement seriously, or their actions are ineffective.

Gallup, which has been tracking employee engagement since 2000, constantly reports employee engagement scores in the U.S. around 32% and at an even more dismal 13% worldwide. Gallup defines engaged employees as those who are involved in, enthusiastic about, and committed to their work and workplace.

Perhaps even worse, the on-going Gallup research into employee engagement also shows a steady rate of actively disengaged employees in the 16% to 18% range at any time. With nearly one in five workers being actively disengaged, it is little wonder that workplace disruption, drama, and conflict are everyday occurrences. Additionally, Gallup estimates that actively disengaged employees cost U.S. businesses $450 billion to $550 billion annually in lost productivity.

Leaders at all levels of organizations should be greatly concerned that roughly 70% of American workers showing up for work uninterested in their jobs, not enthusiastic about their work, or uncommitted to delivering their best performance day in and day out.

The fact that these employee engagement figures have been fairly steady for almost two decades shows that there is a huge gap between leaders knowing about employee disengagement and being successful at creating and executing solutions to this problem.

The cost of employee disengagement is phenomenal. According to Gallup, companies with highly engaged workforces outperform their peers by 147% in earnings per share. These companies also realize on average:

41% fewer quality defects.

48% fewer safety incidents.

28% less shrinkage (employee theft or wastage).

65% less turnover (in low turnover organizations).

25% less turnover (in high turnover organizations).

37% less absenteeism.

As the Gallup survey shows, there are some hefty benefits and savings to be gained from having a highly engaged workforce.

Increasing Employee Engagement

For years managers were taught that employees can be motivated by a mixture of rewards and punishment. I am not sure how true this ever was, but it certainly has about zero validity today.

In my experience as a leader, and from my decades of facilitating leadership development programs, I believe the large majority of people will raise themselves only to a leader's lowest expectation of them.

Thus, the first place to start for improving employee engagement is for the leader to raise their expectations of his or her team members. Leaders have to create an environment where their team members accept the challenge to step up and perform at higher levels. It is the leader's responsibility to drive participation of the people she or he leads.

The corollary to this is that the leader also has to *involve* the team members in determining *how to execute* at higher levels. Employee engagement does not result from a top-down, command-and-control approach. In fact, this style of leadership typically deflates employee engagement and sparks active employee disengagement.

Employee engagement is not rocket science. But it does require placing an organization-wide focus on leading people to achieve results over an emphasis on getting things done and improving productivity ratios.

Increasing employee engagement may be as simple as leaders focusing on the seven things that motivated team members want most:

A sense of purpose, to know they are contributors.

Some amount of autonomy, particularly in deciding how to accomplish a given task.

A safe workplace environment to express their questions and concerns and to learn from mistakes.

Empathy from their supervisors and leaders.

Professional and personal improvement.

Coaching and mentoring.

On-going education opportunities.

Not surprisingly, half of these six items are related to personal development, which is why I say increasing employee engagement is the second top priority for leaders after the development of their team members and direct reports.

Leaders who place a great deal of emphasis on the professional development of their team members are likely to be rewarded with increased employee engagement, as well as more knowledgeable and productive workers.

Some of the best ways to motivate today's workforce are:

Eliminate long-standing stupid rules, procedures, and processes no longer appropriate for today's workforce.

Be flexible in how you lead individuals and team members.

Provide on-going and timely feedback to all team members.

Never act like you are superior or better than your team members simply because you are the boss or the designated leader.

Another great way to motivate employee engagement is to provide every team member with a clear line of sight to their role and importance on a task or project. When a leader's communication provides clarity and understanding, and the leader engages in a dialogue that openly discusses the concerns and questions of other team members, then motivation and buy-in are more likely to occur.

A clear line of sight shows team members how they are contributing to the team or business unit, and how the team or business unit is contributing to the success of the organization. That, combined with some autonomy on how they contribute, goes a long way to increasing employee engagement. After all, no one wants to be micromanaged by their leader. And no leader who wants to increase employee engagement within his or her team will make the mistake of being a micromanager.

Appreciation and Gratitude

The combination of leadership and gratitude is extremely powerful. Yet expressing gratitude is one of the least-utilized skills in the leadership toolbox.

A ten-year, groundbreaking study of 200,000 managers and employees by O.C. Tanner Learning group revealed two startling statistics:

1) 79% of employees who quit their jobs cite a lack of appreciation as a key reason for leaving.

2) 65% of North Americans report that they were not recognized even once by their leaders or supervisors during the last year.

It is little wonder that The Society of Human Resource Management Association (SHRM) says that only 38% of employees feel very satisfied with their current jobs.

One of my pet rules of leadership is: *recognize effort, reward results.*

It is very important to recognize, and to show appreciation for, the efforts being made by team members. Too many leaders and managers only acknowledge and express appreciation for outcomes and results. This is a mistake.

No successful sports coach waits until a game is over before telling players their efforts are on track and benefitting the team. Instead, sports coaches yell out encouragement and accolades throughout the game for hustle, smart decisions, and effort. These are not given just when points are scored or when the other team is prevented from scoring.

The same needs to happen in the workplace. Leaders who express gratitude and appreciation for the *efforts* of team members create a workplace climate where employee engagement is higher, as compared to those leaders who only acknowledge final results and outcomes.

Research cited in numerous books and articles clearly shows that recognition and appreciation are the two things that employees say their bosses could do better that would motivate them to produce better work.

Quotes on Leading Employee Engagement

Paychecks can't buy passion.
Brad Federman

All employees have an innate desire to contribute to something bigger than themselves.
Jag Randhawa

When people go to work, they shouldn't have to leave their hearts at home.
Betty Bender

You can't sell it outside if you can't sell it inside.
Stan Slap

Some companies don't have an engagement problem; they have a hiring problem.
Bob Kelleher

The only way to do great work is to love what you do.
Steve Jobs

The way your employees feel is the way your customers will feel. And if your employees don't feel valued, neither will your customers.
Sybil F. Stershic

When people are financially invested, they want a return. When people are emotionally invested, they want to contribute.
Simon Sinek

Culture is about performance, and making people feel good about how they contribute to the whole.
Tracy Streckenbach

Employee engagement is the art and science of engaging people in authentic and recognized connections to strategy, roles, performance, organization, community, relationship, customers, development, energy, and happiness to leverage, sustain, and transform work into results.
David Zinger

Engaged employees are in the game for the sake of the game; they believe in the cause of the organization.
Paul Marciano

But here's the hard truth of leadership: when leaders display the rarefied strength of valuing their employees, legacies are made, careers advance, and companies ultimately flourish.
Marcel Schwantes

Everyone wants to be appreciated, so if you appreciate someone, don't keep it a secret.
Mary Kay Ash

Highly engaged employees make the customer experience. Disengaged employees break it.
Timothy R. Clark

It's sad, really, how a negative workplace can impact our lives and the way we feel about ourselves. The situation is reaching pandemic heights — most people go to work at jobs they dislike, supervised by people who don't care about them, and directed by senior leaders who are often clueless about where to take the company.
Leigh Branham and Mark Hirschfeld

People leave when they don't feel appreciated. That's why we've made recognition a really high value. Our business is people-capability first; then you satisfy customers; then you make money.
David Novak

The real damper on employee engagement is the soggy, cold blanket of centralized authority. In most companies, power cascades downwards from the CEO. Not only are employees disenfranchised from most policy decisions, they lack even the power to rebel against egocentric and tyrannical supervisors.
Gary Hamel

People want to know they matter and they want to be treated as people. That's the new talent contract.
Pamela Stroko

Dispirited, unmotivated, unappreciated workers cannot compete in a highly competitive world.
Frances Hesselbein

Employees engage with employers and brands when they're treated as humans worthy of respect.
Meghan M. Biro

Engaged employees stay for what they give (they like their work); disengaged employees stay for what they get (favorable job conditions, growth opportunities, job security).
Blessing White's The State of Employee Engagement 2008

I consider my ability to arouse enthusiasm among men the greatest asset I possess. The way to develop the best that is in a man is by appreciation and encouragement.
Charles Schwab

On what high-performing companies should be striving to create: A great place for great people to do great work.
Marilyn Carlson

There are only three measurements that tell you nearly everything you need to know about your organization's overall performance: employee engagement, customer satisfaction, and cash flow.
Jack Welch

TURNED ON people figure out how to beat the competition, TURNED OFF people only complain about being beaten by the competition.
Ben Simonton

You'll attract the employees you need if you can explain why your mission is compelling: not why it's important in general, but why you're doing something important that no one else is going to get done.
Peter Thiel

Connect the dots between individual roles and the goals of the organization. When people see that connection, they get a lot of energy out of work. They feel the importance, dignity, and meaning in their job.
Ken Blanchard

Early in my career, one of the first business lessons I learned was this: It's impossible to win the hearts and minds of people unless you clearly establish goals and values and reward people if they act in a way that leads to the fulfillment of those objectives. It quickly became clear to me that if you want to make sure your customers are treated well, you have to make sure you treat your employees well and recognize their efforts.
F. Robert Salerno

Employees who believe that management is concerned about them as a whole person — not just an employee — are more productive, more satisfied, more fulfilled. Satisfied employees mean satisfied customers, which leads to profitability.
Anne M. Mulcahy

Everyone enjoys doing the kind of work for which he is best suited.
Napoleon Hill

It all came down to employee engagement. It all came down to recognition. It all came down to leadership, which led to every sailor feeling ownership and accountability for the results. You can ask a team to accomplish a mission, but you can't order excellence.
Mike Abrashoff

Research indicates that workers have three prime needs: Interesting work, recognition for doing a good job, and being let in on things that are going on in the company.
Zig Ziglar

You have to want to be engaged. There has to be a deep-seated desire in your heart and mind to participate, to be involved, and to make a difference. If the desire isn't there, no person or book can plant it within you.
Timothy R. Clark

Create caring and robust connections between every employee and their work, customers, leaders, managers, and the organization to achieve results that matter to everyone in this sentence.
David Zinger

Appreciate everything your associates do for the business. Nothing else can quite substitute for a few well-chosen, well-timed, sincere words of praise. They're absolutely free and worth a fortune.
Sam Walton

To build a culture of engagement, it is important to incorporate training on intrinsic motivation and employee engagement into management development programs.
Kenneth Thomas

We think it's important for employees to have fun... it drives employee engagement.
Tony Hsieh

The real art of conversation is not only to say the right thing at the right time, but also to leave unsaid the wrong thing at the tempting moment.
Dorothy Nevill

They may forget what you said, but they will never forget how you made them feel.
Carl W. Buehner

The best of us are those who help the rest of us.
Anthony Douglas Williams

Our chief want is someone who will inspire us to be what we know we could be.
Ralph Waldo Emerson

Be quick to praise people.
Bernard Baruch

Make finding the good in others a priority.
Zig Ziglar

Nothing great was ever achieved without enthusiasm.
Ralph Waldo Emerson

Everyone has an invisible sign hanging from their neck saying "Make me feel important." Never forget this message when working with people.
Mary Kay Ash

All cruelty springs from weakness.
Seneca

Feeling grateful or appreciative of someone or something in your life actually attracts more of the things that you appreciate and value into your life.
Christiane Northrup

Shared joy is a double joy; shared sorrow is half a sorrow.
Swedish Proverb

What is uttered from the heart alone, will win the hearts of others to your own.
Johann Wolfgang von Goethe

What you do not want done to yourself, do not do to others.
Confucius

Never underestimate the difference YOU can make in the lives of others.
Pablo (James Gregory Paul Sr.)

The strong forgive, the weak remember.
Ecuadorian Proverb

We will try to create conditions where people can come together in a spirit of teamwork, and exercise to their heart's desire their technological capacity.
Akio Morita

Celebrate what you want to see more of.
Tom Peters

Recompense injury with justice, recompense kindness with kindness.
Confucius

Make no judgments where you have no compassion.
Anne McCaffrey

How much easier is it to be generous than just.
Junius

Judge a man by his questions rather than his answers.
Voltaire

The magic formula that successful businesses have discovered is to treat customers like guests and employees like people.
Tom Peters

If people are good only because they fear punishment, and hope for reward, then we are a sorry lot indeed.
Albert Einstein

Surround yourself with great people; delegate authority; get out of the way.
Ronald Reagan

I would rather try to persuade a man to go along, because once I have persuaded him he will stick. If I scare him, he will stay just as long as he is scared, and then he is gone.
Dwight D. Eisenhower

Winning isn't always championships.
Michael Jordan

If you would persuade, you must appeal to interest rather than intellect.
Benjamin Franklin

It is much more valuable to look for the strength in others. You can gain nothing by criticizing their imperfections.
Daisaku Ikeda

Don't find fault — find a remedy.
Henry Ford

Instruction does much, but encouragement everything.
Johann Wolfgang von Goethe

People lose their way when they lose their why.
Michael Hyatt

Sometimes a player's greatest challenge is coming to grips with his role on the team.
Scottie Pippen

I have a rule on my team: When we talk to one another, we look each other right in the eye, because I think it's tough to lie to somebody. You give respect to somebody.
Mike Krzyzewski

Sharing emotions builds deeper relationships. Motivation comes from working on things we care about.
Sheryl Sandberg

There's a difference between interest and commitment. When you're interested in doing something, you do it only when circumstances permit. When you're committed to something, you accept no excuses, only results.
Art Turock

People rarely succeed unless they have fun in what they are doing.
Dale Carnegie

Feeling gratitude and not expressing it is like wrapping a present and not giving it.
William Arthur Ward

When feedback is combined with forgiveness leaders are more likely to prompt and motivate changes that result in better performance and improved behavior.
Steven B. Howard

I would maintain that thanks are the highest form of thought; and that gratitude is happiness doubled by wonder.
G. K. Chesterton

Silent gratitude isn't very much to anyone.
Gertrude Stein

Thankfulness is the beginning of gratitude. Gratitude is the completion of thankfulness. Thankfulness may consist merely of words. Gratitude is shown in acts.
Henri Frederic Amiel

Enthusiasm releases the drive to carry you over obstacles and adds significance to all you do.
Norman Vincent Peale

Gratitude is a currency that we can mint for ourselves, and spend without fear of bankruptcy.
Fred De Witt Van Amburgh

The deepest craving of human nature is the need to be appreciated.
William James

An idea that excites, ignites.
Ron Kaufman

Don't forget, a person's greatest emotional need is to feel appreciated.
H. Jackson Brown Jr.

People leave when they don't feel appreciated. That's why we've made recognition a really high value. Our business is people-capability first; then you satisfy customers; then you make money.
David Novak

Connect the dots between individual roles and the goals of the organization. When people see that connection, they get a lot of energy out of work. They feel the importance, dignity, and meaning in their job.
Ken Blanchard

For most of them, it can be summed up by one of four things: They love what they do (their job), they love the Disney brand (their organization), they love their manager (their boss), or they love the people they work with (their squad).
Peter Blank

CHAPTER 7

Leading For Results

G reat leaders drive results by focusing on four skills and behaviors:

Communicating as a leader.

Ensuring individual and team accountability.

Developing clear and concise strategy statements.

Leveraging cross-functional and cross-cultural collaboration.

One of my core leadership beliefs is that leaders can be found at all levels of an organization. Leadership is not something confined to the upper ranks of management or the top tiers of an organization chart.

Likewise, strategy is not something done only at the corporate or strategic business unit level. Any leader can have a strategy, such as:

A customer retention strategy.

A service quality strategy.

An innovation strategy.

A new product strategy.

A cost-reduction strategy.

A leadership development strategy.

A team development strategy.

However, setting a strategy or a vision for your workgroup is never sufficient in itself. Far too many strategies fail to achieve their intended outcomes. I'll share with you later in this chapter some of the main reasons why strategic plans fail.

Setting Strategic Direction

A strategy is simply a vision of going from a current situation to a desired state, complete with actionable plans and identified resources. But while this may sound simple, in reality most strategies are anything but simple. In addition, as Jedi Master Yoda teaches us, *"Difficult to see. Always in motion is the future."*

When created in the upper echelons of organizations, strategies tend to be convoluted, cross-functional, big picture in scope, and longer term in outlook and completion tenure. When created at the coalface of operations, strategies tend to be tactical and short-term in nature and usually aimed at solving a single specific problem or challenge.

Mid-level leaders are often tasked with taking strategies developed above and creating tactics and plans to accomplish the assigned goals and objectives. This is why I often refer to mid-level leaders as *the glue between strategy and execution.*

At all levels strategies must provide a clear roadmap for where the leader wants the organization or team to go, the resources available to get there, and the reasons why it is important to move in the stated direction and toward the desired outcome.

It is the leader's responsibility to determine the destination and desired state for which the strategy and action plans will be designed. You may involve others in the formulation of your strategies, but my advice is to keep such groups small and highly focused. Too much involvement and participation of others at the strategy development stage can cause unnecessary delays, a slower process, and even paralysis by analysis.

If it takes too long to develop a strategy, or to execute it, the desired results may be missed. Those who hesitate often lose out to more nimble and swifter competitors. That is not something you ever want to have to tell or explain to your bosses, or even your team members.

Remember any strategy is a living thing. You can course correct or make modifications in execution any time you sense you and your team have gone off track. As long as you keep the final destination and the desired results in mind, changes in execution are okay. It's like sailing, you have to tack and change your sail configuration whenever the wind changes.

On the other hand, do not lead by the seat of your pants. Great leaders are those with strategies, execution plans, and resources in hand.

Why Strategic Plans Fail

Research shows that over 70% of all change initiatives worldwide fail to achieve their intended results. Surprisingly, this figure has remained fairly constant for several decades.

Why are organizations so poor at implementing strategic plans?

One key reason, according to Bridges Business Consulting International, is that "leadership teams habitually underestimate the implementation challenge and what is involved." In our estimation, this really goes back to the leadership team creating the executional "hows" rather than involving the frontline implementers in helping to craft the executional tactics and plans.

Too often the post-mortems on failed strategies reveal these causes:

- The strategy is often set by those who do not have to execute it.

- The strategy is frequently set by those who do not understand how to execute it.

- Strategies are often overly optimistic on what is required to execute successfully.

- Leaders want strategies executed immediately, or as quickly as possible, without understanding the ramifications of expedited deadlines.

- Leaders who fall in love with their own ideas and plans without fully understanding what it takes to implement those ideas and plans.

As you can see, it is often the way leaders approach problems, and how they determine the solutions required, that often cause strategic plans to go astray.

There are many other reasons why strategic plans fail. Here are 10 of the most prominent ones:

1) Unrealistic goals.

2) Lack of focus and resources.

3) Plans that are overly complex.

4) Financial estimates that are significantly inaccurate (and usually overly optimistic).

5) Plans based on insufficient data.

6) Inflexible or undefined team roles and responsibilities (often leading to confusion, inaction or wrong steps).

7) Staffing requirements not fully understood.

8) Project scope is inflexible with no room to meet changing conditions.

9) Leaders believe the hardest part is creating the strategy, when in fact implementation is the hardest part.

10) Leaders do not communicate clearly and frequently.

Great leaders will provide an overview of how to achieve the strategic objectives, but leave the details of the "how" to those executing the strategy. Average leaders, on the other hand, are more likely to develop and include the details of execution in their strategic plans, forcing the execution teams to follow a designated path. This methodology has a lower degree of successful execution than the process used by great leaders.

Collaboration

Collaboration between individuals, departments, work groups, colleagues, outside contractors, and even between peer-level leaders, is essential in today's world.

Hence, leaders are also accountable for ensuring that collaboration takes place between all team members and work groups, as well as between themselves and others.

Collaboration means working together to attain a shared outcome. The key word here is shared.

Collaboration is not about getting others to help achieve your own goals or objectives. There must be benefits to both parties (or to all parties when multi-group collaboration is necessary), though these benefits need not be equal in size, stature, or importance.

Also, collaboration does not mean compromise. One party making a compromise does not equate to collaboration. There is a huge difference between asking another person or department to compromise and asking them to collaborate.

Successful collaboration comes from a strong mixture of three factors:

Shared goals and outcomes.

Influence skills.

Handing collaboration conflict.

Shared goals and outcomes, of course, is part of the very definition of collaboration. The other two factors are leadership skills that need to be learned and honed.

Collaboration works best when there are "big picture" results for customers and the organization. Conflict often ensues when the perceived results overly benefit either customers or the organization. The same is true when a collaboration project on internal processes, policies, or procedures greatly favors one part of the organization over another or all others.

Interestingly, it is actually easier for siloed members of an organization to collaborate in times of major stress or in a crises situation. This is because internal barriers and silos come crashing down when an "all hands on deck" situation occurs. Sadly, people tend to go back to their old non-collaborative ways once the crises or urgency is over.

Unfortunately, the silo mentality and the various rewards and recognition systems in most organizations often prevent routine collaboration between team members and peers from happening. Very few organizations rank their team members on their ability to collaborate (despite this being a critical success skill). Likewise, few individual performance goals used in annual performance reviews are based on collaborative results or outcomes.

When such systemic hurdles are in place, it is up to leaders (at all levels) to pro-actively engage in collaboration for the good of their teams, the organization as a whole, or even themselves. Doing so is the hallmark of a great leader, even when the results may not directly impact promotion and bonuses. Doing so will, however, impact results and how the leader is perceived by team members, direct reports, and peers.

Quotes on Leading For Results

It is more important to know where you are going than to get there quickly. Do not mistake activity for achievement.
Isocrates

The vision must be followed by the venture. It is not enough to stare up the steps. We must step up the stairs.
Vance Havner

Goals. There's no telling what you can do when you get inspired by them. There's no telling what you can do when you believe in them. There's no telling what will happen when you act upon them.
Jim Rohn

The most important key to achieving great success is to decide upon your goal and launch, get started, take action, move.
John Wooden

Determination gives you the resolve to keep going in spite of the roadblocks that lay before you.
Denis Waitley

The five essential entrepreneurial skills for success are concentration, discrimination, organization, innovation and communication.
Michael Faraday

Start by doing what is necessary; then do what's possible; and suddenly you're doing the impossible.
Saint Francis of Assisi

The way to get started is to quit talking and begin doing.
Walt Disney

Don't wait. The time will never be just right.
Napoleon Hill

Perhaps the very best question that you can memorize and repeat, over and over, is, "what is the most valuable use of my time right now?"
Brian Tracy

Stay committed to your decisions, but stay flexible in your approach.
Anthony Robbins

Follow effective actions with quiet reflection. From the quiet reflection will come even more effective action.
Peter Drucker

Setting a goal is not the main thing. It is deciding how you will go about achieving it and staying with that plan.
Tom Landry

Make failure your teacher, not your undertaker.
Zig Ziglar

Don't tell people how to do things, tell them what to do and let them surprise you with their results.
George S. Patton

The mark of a great man is one who knows when to set aside the important things in order to accomplish the vital ones.
Brandon Sanderson

Always remember, Son, the best boss is the one who bosses the least. Whether it's cattle, or horses, or men; the least government is the best government.
Ralph Moody

I cannot give you a formula for success, but I can give you the formula for failure, which is: try to please everybody.
Herbert Bayard Swope

It is a mistake to think that moving fast is the same as actually going somewhere.
Steve Goodier

Consensus: The process of abandoning all beliefs, principles, values, and policies in search of something in which no one believes, but to which no one objects; the process of avoiding the very issues that have to be solved, merely because you cannot get agreement on the way ahead. What great cause would have been fought and won under the banner "I stand for consensus?"
Margaret Thatcher

Failure is the opportunity to begin again more intelligently.
Henry Ford

Sometimes, you are not prepared for the event but the event prepares you.
Howard Schultz

Spend 80 percent of your time focusing on the opportunities of tomorrow rather than the problems of yesterday.
Brian Tracy

Aim for success, not perfection. Never give up your right to be wrong, because then you will lose the ability to learn new things and move forward with your life.
David M. Burns

Great leaders are not afraid of mistakes or failure. They are only afraid of not learning from mistakes and failure.
Steven B. Howard

The secret of success is to go from failure to failure without any loss of enthusiasm.
Winston Churchill

If the only tool you have is a hammer, you tend to see every problem as a nail.
Abraham Maslow

Work is effort applied toward some end. The most satisfying work involves directing our efforts toward achieving ends that we ourselves endorse as worthy expressions of our talent and character.
William Bennett

The ability to discipline yourself to delay gratification in the short term in order to enjoy greater rewards in the long term is the indispensable prerequisite for success.
Brian Tracy

The difference in winning and losing is most often, not quitting.
Walt Disney

Effective people are not problem-minded; they are opportunity-minded. They feed opportunities and starve problems.
Stephen Covey

Everyone who has ever taken a shower has had an idea. It's the person who gets out of the shower, dries off and does something about it that makes a difference.
Nolan Bushnell

Done is better than perfect.
Sheryl Sandberg

Efficiency is doing the thing right. Effectiveness is doing the right thing.
Peter Drucker

A goal is not always meant to be reached; it often serves simply as something to aim at.
Bruce Lee

Ideas are completely, completely, completely worthless unless you execute against those ideas. And you can sit here and tell me what your "purpose" is, but unless you go and execute against it, it is not different than an idea, which is completely useless without fundamental execution.
Gary Vaynerchuk

Remember that failure is an event, not a person.
Zig Ziglar

A good plan violently executed now is better than a perfect plan executed next week.
George S. Patton

You cannot expect victory and plan for defeat.
Joel Osteen

Insanity is doing the same thing, over and over again, but expecting different results.
Albert Einstein

As competition intensifies, the need for creative thinking increases. It is no longer enough to do the same thing better, no longer enough to be efficient and solve problems.
Edward de Bono

Many people fail in life, not for lack of ability or brains or even courage but simply because they have never organized their energies around a goal.
Elbert Hubbard

The key is not to prioritize your schedule but to schedule your priorities.
Stephen Covey

Our goals can only be reached through a vehicle of a plan, in which we must fervently believe, and upon which we must vigorously act. There is no other route to success.
Stephen A. Brennan

If you want something new, you have to stop doing something old.
Peter Drucker

We keep moving forward, opening new doors, and doing new things, because we're curious, and curiosity keeps leading us down new paths.
Walt Disney

It is not enough to be busy; so are the ants. The question is: What are we busy about?
Henry David Thoreau

We can't solve problems by using the same kind of thinking we used when we created them.
Albert Einstein

Most of the important things in the world have been accomplished by people who have kept on trying when there seemed to be no hope at all.
Dale Carnegie

Be not afraid of going slowly. Be afraid only of standing still.
Chinese Proverb

If you decide that you're going to do only the things you know are going to work, you're going to leave a lot of opportunity on the table.
Jeff Bezos

Only those who dare to fail greatly can ever achieve greatly.
Robert F. Kennedy

Most of us spend too much time on what is urgent and not enough time on what is important.
Stephen Covey

If you want to make an easy job seem mighty hard, just keep putting off doing it.
Olin Miller

Don't judge each day by the harvest you reap, but by the seeds you plant.
Robert Louis Stevenson

Nothing is so fatiguing as the eternal hanging on of an uncompleted task.
William James

Much of the stress that people feel doesn't come from having too much to do. It comes from not finishing what they started.
David Allen

Finish each day and be done with it. You have done what you could. Some blunders and absurdities no doubt crept in, forget them as soon as you can. Tomorrow is a new day, you shall begin it well and serenely.
Ralph Waldo Emerson

Obstacles are those frightful things you see when you take your eyes off your goals.
Henry Ford

Tomorrow is often the busiest day of the week.
Spanish Proverb

Worry often gives a small thing a big shadow.
Swedish Proverb

A year from now you may wish you had started today.
Karen Lamb

Progress is less about speed and much more about direction.
Steven B. Howard

Nothing destroys a good idea faster than a mandatory consensus.
Jessica Hagy

Failure is a detour, not a dead-end street.
Zig Ziglar

Defeat is a state of mind; No one is ever defeated until defeat has been accepted as a reality.
Bruce Lee

The person who removes a mountain begins by carrying away small stones.
Chinese Proverb

You have to decide what your highest priorities are and have the courage — pleasantly, smilingly, non-apologetically — to say 'no' to other things. And the way to do that is by having a bigger 'yes' burning inside.
Stephen Covey

Always focus on accomplishments rather than activities.
Brian Tracy

It is a mistake to think that moving fast is the same as actually going somewhere.
Steve Goodier

He who establishes his argument by noise and command shows that his reason is weak.
Michel de Montaigne

A clear vision, backed by definite plans, gives you a tremendous feeling of confidence and personal power.
Brian Tracy

Weak desires bring weak results, just as a small amount of fire brings a small amount of heat.
Napoleon Hill

We always plan too much and always think too little.
Joseph Schumpeter

Without deviation from the norm, "progress" is not possible.
Frank Zappa

Nothing will ever be attempted if all possible objections must first be overcome.
Samuel Johnson

Talk doesn't cook rice.
Chinese Proverb

It is much easier to propose than to execute.
David Noonan

To think too long about doing a thing often becomes its undoing.
Eva Young

Nothing is less productive than to make more efficient what should not be done at all.
Peter Drucker

The victory of success is half won when one gains the habit of setting goals and achieving them. Even the most tedious chore will become endurable as you parade through each day convinced that every task, no matter how menial or boring, brings you closer to fulfilling your dreams.
Og Mandino

Don't let the fear of the time it will take to accomplish something stand in the way of your doing it. The time will pass anyway; we might just as well put that passing time to the best possible use.
Earl Nightingale

It's how you deal with failure that determines how you achieve success.
David Feherty

It is our attitude at the beginning of a difficult task that, more than anything else, will affect its successful outcome.
William James

Satisfaction lies in the effort, not in the attainment. Full effort is full victory.
Mohandas Karamchand (Mahatma) Gandhi

Goals provide the energy source that powers our lives. One of the best ways we can get the most from the energy we have is to focus it. That is what goals can do for us; concentrate our energy.
Denis Waitley

It's not that I'm so smart, it's just that I stay with problems longer.
Albert Einstein

Good is the enemy of great.
Jim Collins

Don't confuse progress with winning.
Mary Barra

Luck is what happens when preparation meets opportunity.
Seneca

You don't get any medal for trying something, you get medals for results.
Bill Parcells

Your positive action combined with positive thinking results in success.
Shiv Khera

You don't get results by focusing on results. You get results by focusing on the actions that produce results.
Mike Hawkins

Culture drives great results.
Jack Welch

You don't concentrate on the risks. You concentrate on results. No risk is too great to prevent the necessary job from getting done.
Chuck Yeager

Superhuman effort isn't worth a damn unless it achieves results.
Ernest Shackleton

The results you achieve will be in direct proportion to the effort you apply.
Denis Waitley

I have a foundational belief that business results start with culture and your people.
Douglas Conant

Business and human endeavors are systems. We tend to focus on snapshots of isolated parts of the system. And wonder why our deepest problems never get solved
Peter Senge

Knowledge is a process of piling up facts; wisdom lies in their simplification.
Martin H. Fischer

The way to get started is to quit talking and begin doing.
Walt Disney

The way to get things done is not to mind who gets the credit for doing them.
Benjamin Jowett

Nothing kills a good idea like a committee.
Jessica Hagy

It is a capital mistake to theorize before one has data.
Sir Arthur Conan Doyle

Wisdom equals knowledge plus courage. You have to not only know what to do and when to do it, but you have to also be brave enough to follow through.
Jarod Kintz

You must learn to translate wisdom and strong feelings into labor.
Jim Rohn

Take time to deliberate; but when the time for action arrives, stop thinking and go in.
Napoleon Bonaparte

Ideas are like rabbits. You get a couple, learn how to handle them, and pretty soon you have a dozen.
John Steinbeck

The way to get good ideas is to get lots of ideas, and throw the bad ones away.
Linus Pauling

By failing to prepare, you are preparing to fail.
Benjamin Franklin

The majority of men meet with failure because of their lack of persistence in creating new plans to take the place of those which fail.
Napoleon Hill

Don't base your desired outcome on income. Do some good.
Steven B. Howard

Concentrate all your thoughts upon the work at hand. The sun's rays do not burn until brought to a focus.
Alexander Graham Bell

Have a bias toward action. Let's see something happen now. You can break that big plan into small steps and take the first step right way.
Indira Gandhi

We often discover what will do, by finding out what will not do; and probably he who never made a mistake never made a discovery.
Samuel Smiles

That which we persist in doing becomes easier, not that the nature of the task has changed, but our ability to do has increased.
Ralph Waldo Emerson

Ask not what the cost of doing this will be. Ask what the cost of not doing it will be.
Rear Admiral Grace Murray Hopper

CHAPTER 8

Ensuring Accountability

W hen leaders talk about ensuring accountability they are usually referring to practices such as holding people accountable for results.

Good leaders take this a step further by emphasizing that accountability is about more than just results. They hold both themselves and others accountable for the decisions and options producing the results, as well as for the actual outcomes. A good leader will also hold herself or himself accountable for utilizing the right level of delegation when appropriately empowering team members.

In addition to these responsibilities, great leaders tend to have a larger organizational perspective, thus holding themselves and others accountable for how their decisions and actions impact other departments and business units as well as customers and business partners.

Great leaders also go even further by holding themselves and other leaders accountable for their leadership behaviors, actions, and for making ethical decisions. I call this Leadership Accountability.

Leadership Accountability

Leadership Accountability is not just about owning up to mistakes or ensuring that processes and procedures are followed faithfully. Leadership Accountability is being true to the purpose and values that drive the organization.

This type of leadership accountability means that personal and departmental agendas are put aside for the greater good and sustainable health of the organization.

At the heart of Leadership Accountability is trust.

Trust is more than the leader being held accountable for doing what they say they will do. Trust also means the leader will make decisions based on what is best for the entire organization, its customers, and the world we live in.

Great leaders build trust through transparency and honesty. They are willing to explain the reasons behind decisions. They are also willing to acknowledge when they do not know the answer or solution to a problem.

Long gone are the days when leaders should never exhibit weakness or vulnerability in front of their team members. Doing so does not cause staff and direct reports to question or doubt your leadership skills. It causes them to see you as human, and as someone struggling with some of the same issues and concerns they are. It is archaic and utter nonsense to think otherwise.

Without a doubt, leaders need to be strong and exhibit resilience, especially during a crisis situation or in particularly difficult and trying times. Such exhibition of strength and displays of resilience will be appreciated and admired by your team members when you and your team are facing enormous challenges and demanding situations.

However, there are appropriate situations and times when, in a positive and forthcoming way, and with the right audience, leaders can admit their vulnerabilities, blind spots, uncertainties, and weaknesses.

In doing so, great leaders become trusted by their followers. Such trust enables followers and other team members to be more willing to raise problems and concerns with their leaders, allowing problems to be dealt with sooner when they are more manageable.

Without trust, no aspect of your leadership philosophy or leadership mindset matters. Without trust your leadership philosophy, mindset, and beliefs are simply invalid and unlikely to be accepted by others.

Every leader makes mistakes. Great leaders readily acknowledge their errors and mistakes. And not just to themselves! They own up and admit slipups, blunders, incorrect decisions, miscalculations, and poor leadership behavior to their colleagues, peers, and direct reports. Average leaders tend to ignore, brush over, or cover up their occasional mistakes, often in the hopes that nobody has noticed. Believe me, they have!

Here are the types of mistakes that leaders make that break the bonds of trust:

- Showing favoritism to one or more team members.

- Withholding information on purpose to keep others, particularly peers, out of the loop or misinformed.

- Showing up unannounced at a meeting being led by a direct report.

- Taking credit for the work of your team without sharing the credit.

- Giving feedback in anger.

- Gossiping or spreading knowingly false stories about colleagues.

- Demanding someone do something simply because you're the boss.

- Not recognizing efforts of team members and considering extra efforts to merely be "part of the job requirement."

- Frequently missing or being late to meetings with team members simply because you're the (very busy) boss, thus not respecting their time, their workloads, and their commitments to others.

- Not keeping promises and commitments.

- Making vague, general promises and commitments that you know team members perceive as more rock solid, especially when it concerns their career advancement opportunities.

All of these are easy mistakes to make in the hustle and bustle of the day. But while they may seem like minor infractions, each is a trust buster; especially when they become frequent leadership behaviors.

Great leadership is a mixture of vulnerability, humility, self-confidence, forgiveness, ethical judgment, and a personal code upon which to based leadership behaviors and actions.

It takes all this, and more, to consistently hold yourself and others accountable for all leadership behaviors, actions, and decisions.

When Leadership Accountability is absent, as we have seen at Volkswagen, Enron, HSBC, Wells Fargo, the U.S. Veterans Administration, and other organizations, devastating disasters and ethical crises often arise. In some instances, neither the brand nor the organization recovers from Leadership Accountability lapses.

Accountability Happens By Design

Accountability in an organization does not happen by including it is the corporate values statement, producing a brochure on corporate values, or by placing posters on the walls with definitions of accountability.

For proof of this, look at our current global benchmark for corporate cheating scandals: Volkswagen. At the time of their deliberate attempt to circumvent the U.S. Clean Air Act by installing cheat device software in over a half million Volkswagen, Audi, and Porsche cars exported to the United States, Volkswagen had a well-written and detailed 24-page Corporate Conduct Guidelines book that did nothing to prevent or stop deliberate cheating and fraudulent actions.

Leaders at every level of an organization must model accountability and deliver on their own commitments to team members, peers, and bosses. In addition, leaders must also hold all others in the organization accountable.

This can be difficult as it is not easy confronting a co-worker whose actions, decisions, or behaviors have exceeded corporate, legal, or moral boundaries. Some might fear that having a culture of holding people accountable might create an unwanted culture of blaming, naming, and shaming.

However, if you want to ensure a culture of accountability, you have to hold people accountable for their actions, decisions, and behaviors. This can be done in a non-confrontational way, especially if you approach each incident with an attitude that your purpose in holding a person accountable is to help develop them and help them improve their workplace performance (instead of an attitude of it's time to punish or discipline the person).

This works best when leaders tell their team members up front that they are going to be held accountable. At the same time, leaders should also describe the process for how lapses in meeting agreed upon standards will be dealt with. Following through using the described process in a non-threatening way reinforces your personal leadership commitment to accountability and often results in team members holding one another accountable as well.

Advocating For What Is Right

Senior leaders and executives often realize that they are not in the best position to identify and know all the challenges involved in strategy execution. Unfortunately, too many leaders have mindsets and fears of inadequacies that prevent them readily admitting this. As such they do not solicit ideas and inputs from others, nor do they appear willingly receptive to unsolicited ideas and inputs.

As a result, in far too many organizations there is a culture of reluctance within the lower leadership ranks to raise concerns and red flags with more senior colleagues or more experienced team members. This is even more prevalent when team members are from hierarchical cultures such as those found in North Asia, China, parts of Latin America, and Eastern Europe.

Leaders can only change this culture of reluctance by being seen as open to suggestions, questions, and even push-back by their followers and peers. Only a *walk the talk* solution will result in the desired culture change, and it will not happen overnight.

Great leaders devote a significant amount of energy and time to clarifying and understanding the perspectives, ideas, concerns, and questions of others (particularly of those that they lead). Additionally, great leaders do not see clarification questions from team members, peers, or others as a sign of push-back or dissension. In fact, they appreciate such questions and inputs, knowing full well that open and honest dialogues are a key builder of trust.

Likewise, great leaders will also demonstrate confidence and courage when providing feedback to their own bosses and other senior leaders. They also assert their right to express their viewpoints, concerns, and questions in a professional manner.

This is particularly important for mid-level leaders tasked with implementing the strategies handed down from above. Mid-level leaders need to become strong advocates for what is right (and what is truly achievable) by advising senior leaders on what is required to successfully implement a strategic plan. Otherwise, as seen in the previous chapter, strategic plans are more likely to fail to meet stated objectives and results.

Admittedly, advocating for what is right is not always easy to do. It is, however, a key differentiator between a good manager and a great leader. This is especially true when trust, openness, and honesty have not been mutually established between leaders operating at different levels within an organization. However, it is not impossible to do so.

Corporate Social Accountability

Let's start with a basic premise: every organization, and in fact every individual, has the obligation to make the world a better place for our children and grandchildren to inherit.

It's that simple.

It is also a huge responsibility.

From a corporate perspective, this is augmented by short-term responsibilities to four specific sets of stakeholders: customers, employees, shareholders, and the communities in which the organization operates.

Much like the racial segregation and marriage equality laws that have evolved in recent decades, the moral compass on corporate responsibility continues to evolve.

This progression is created by a combination of societal pressures, changing social values and mores, and an increasingly more knowledgeable and frustrated global population. Added to this combustible mix is an increasingly active citizenry that does not hesitate to punish or correct organizations deemed to be outside the boundaries of proper corporate citizenship.

We even see organizations themselves now taking stands against other organizations negatively impacting the world, for instance:

> Starbucks committing to 100% ethically sourced coffee and tea in a global program that aims to positively impact the lives and livelihoods of farmers and their communities.

> Intel committing to use minerals from "conflict-free" sources in the Congo so that their purchases of such minerals do not fund the militant violence and human-rights atrocities in the Democratic Republic of the Congo.

> Grocery chain NTUC FairPrice in Singapore removing products from its shelves made by the company suspected of being involved in the burning of forests in Indonesia which caused an unhealthy smoke haze to descend upon Singapore for weeks.

There can be little doubt, therefore, that Corporate Responsibility is one of the pillars of sustainable success for any organization or corporate entity.

The key word here is sustainable.

Many organizations pay public and internal lip service to the concept of Corporate Social Responsibility. And many get away with this for years and years. But if they do wrong, at some point they will get caught and then disaster strikes.

Witness the recent events surrounding the Volkswagen saga, and the direct impact on three of its four key constituents.

First, employees. Volkswagen employs over 580,000 people worldwide. Let's assume that its diesel engine cars would not have met EPA emission standards in the USA without the company resorting to the cheating it engaged in. That obviously would have resulted in reduced sales, and probably led to a reduced workforce.

So can cheating be condoned when it is perceived to be in the best interest of employees and shareholders?

Such a mentality treats the concept of "best interest" on a short-term thinking basis. And all it does is postpone the inevitable. Workers who would have been fired if car sales declined are now likely to be laid off as the impact of this scandal cascades.

The same goes for shareholders. Short-term holders of shares in Volkswagen benefitted over the seven years while this cheating was being perpetuated. When this saga first unfolded, the share price of Volkswagen was down 40% within just a few weeks. So while one set of shareholders may have benefitted (temporarily), the entire shareholder base is now negatively and massively impacted. One can only hope that this latter group includes all those involved in executing and covering up this duplicitous scandal.

How important is Corporate Responsibility to consumers?

The most recent Edelman goodpurpose™ Consumer Study of 6,000 people in 10 countries showed that an increasing number of people are spending on brands that have a social purpose.

As the survey notes, 66% of the respondents in these 10 countries no longer believe it is good enough for corporations and brands to merely give money away to charitable causes. The belief now is that, to be authentic, corporations and brands must truly integrate good causes into their day-to-day business activities, as well as into their internal processes and procedures.

In another Edelman survey, called the Trust Barometer, 80% of the more than 33,000 people surveyed worldwide said they expect businesses to both make money and improve economic and social conditions in their countries. In addition, 67% felt that businesses are too focused on short-term financial gains, while 57% felt that businesses are not focused enough on their long-term impact on society.

This takes the importance of Corporate Responsibility and Corporate Accountability to a new level.

Going back to the Volkswagen saga. Many current and potential customers of Volkswagen are undoubtedly looking elsewhere for their next vehicle purchase. Reduced sales will impact the VW labor force, its car dealership network, and even its suppliers of materials and parts.

Volkswagen as a corporate entity — which means both its leadership team as well as every employee with knowledge of these shenanigans — had a responsibility to their customers, fellow employees (and their families), the dealer network owners and employees (and their families), and the owners and employees of all its materials and parts suppliers (and their families).

Volkswagen — meaning its leadership team and the employees with knowledge of this deliberate subterfuge — failed to live up to their collective and individual responsibilities to these stakeholders and their families. There was no Leadership Accountability to be seen anywhere within the Volkswagen organization, a fact that has now cost the company over $25 billion and seen two of its employees in the United States sentenced to lengthy terms in federal prison.

In society, when people do not live up to their collective and individual responsibilities to the community, they are usually jailed, ostracized, or outcast.

In the corporate world, such failure to meet the duties of corporate responsibility and leadership accountability results in massive loss of value, reputation, market share, and, of course, sustainable success.

Quotes on Ensuring Accountability

Authority without wisdom is like a heavy ax without an edge, fitter to bruise than polish.
Anne Bradstreet

None of us can hope to get anywhere without character, moral courage and the spiritual strength to accept responsibility.
Thomas J. Watson

When I've heard all I need to make a decision, I don't take a vote. I make a decision.
Ronald Reagan

You cannot create long-term value for the shareholder unless you create long-term value for the employees and the communities you serve.
Howard Schultz

If you trade your authenticity for safety, you may experience the following: anxiety, depression, eating disorders, addiction, rage, blame, resentment, and inexplicable grief.
Brené Brown

We are all accountable for our actions; their affect and influence on our lives and the lives of others.
Sameh Elsayed

Real integrity is doing the right thing, knowing that nobody's going to know whether you did it or not.
Oprah Winfrey

No legacy is so rich as honesty.
Shakespeare

Character is doing the right thing when nobody's looking. There are too many people who think that the only thing that's right is to get by, and the only thing that's wrong is to get caught.
J. C. Watts

Our integrity is the basis of our confidence in ourselves and the confidence we inspire in others.
Stephen Covey

Good character is not formed in a week or a month. It is created little by little, day by day. Protracted and patient effort is needed to develop good character.
Heraclitus

Man must cease attributing his problems to his environment, and learn again to exercise his will – his personal responsibility.
Albert Einstein

Have the courage to say no. Have the courage to face the truth. Do the right thing because it is right. These are the magic keys to living your life with integrity.
W. Clement Stone

Hold yourself responsible for a higher standard than anybody expects of you. Never excuse yourself.
Henry Ward Beecher

Life is the acceptance of responsibilities or their evasion, it is a business of meeting obligations or avoiding them. To every man the choice is continually being offered, and by the manner of his choosing you may fairly measure him.
Ben Ames Williams

Principle — particularly moral principle — can never be a weathervane, spinning around this way and that with the shifting winds of expediency. Moral principle is a compass forever fixed and forever true.
Edward R. Lyman

Justice is conscience, not a personal conscience but the conscience of the whole of humanity. Those who clearly recognize the voice of their own conscience usually recognize also the voice of justice.
Alexander Solzhenitsyn

All labor that up lifts humanity has dignity and importance and should be undertaken with painstaking excellence.
Martin Luther King Jr.

Freedom is the right to be wrong, not the right to do wrong.
John Diefenbaker

Let no man turn aside, ever so slightly, from the broad path of honor, on the plausible pretense that he is justified by the goodness of his end. All good ends can be worked out by good means.
Charles Dickens

One of life's most painful moments comes when we must admit that we didn't do our homework, that we are not prepared.
Merlin Olsen

Because we live in an environment inundated by human doing, more than human being, it's easy to get caught up in imbalance to the point that it no longer reflects mission or principles.
Stephen Covey

A professional is a person who can do his best at a time when he doesn't particularly feel like it.
Alistair Cooke

Right actions for the future are the best apologies for wrong ones in the past.
Tyron Edwards

What is morally wrong can never be advantageous, even when it enables you to make some gain that you believe to be to your advantage. The mere act of believing that some wrongful course of action constitutes an advantage is pernicious.
Marcus Tullius Cicero

What is the nature of true morality? I have argued that it must be a kind of ethics involving letting go of one's own interest on behalf of others, being ready if necessary to sacrifice one's own interests for them, even on behalf of an enemy.
George Ellis

You should never let your fears prevent you from doing what you know is right.
Aung San Suu Kyi

The things that will destroy us are: politics without principle; pleasure without conscience; wealth without work; knowledge without character; business without morality; science without humanity, and worship without sacrifice.
Mohandas Karamchand (Mahatma) Gandhi

Circumstances do not make a man, they reveal him.
Wayne Dyer

The time is always right to do what is right.
Martin Luther King Jr.

Every choice you make has an end result.
Zig Ziglar

The role of business is to make the world a better place for everyone.
Kevin Roberts

The keys to brand success are self-definition, transparency, authenticity, and accountability.
Simon Mainwaring

Integrity is a bargain. It costs a little bit more going in, yet it pays for itself many, many times over. Forget about cutting corners. Do it right and you'll be the one to claim the biggest prize.
Ralph Marston

The power of principles is that they're universal, timeless truths. If we understand and live our lives based on principles, we can quickly adapt; we can apply them anywhere.
Stephen Covey

If anyone can show me, and prove to me, that I am wrong in thought or deed, I will gladly change. I seek the truth, which never yet hurt anybody. It is only persistence in self-delusion and ignorance which does harm.
Marcus Aurelius

Integrity has no need of rules.
Albert Camus

Freedom is not worth having if it does not connote freedom to err. It passes my comprehension how human beings, be they ever so experienced and able, can delight in depriving other human beings of that precious right.
Mohandas Karamchand (Mahatma) Gandhi

Let us put our minds together and see what life we can make for our children.
Sitting Bull

I have found that the greatest help in meeting any problem with decency and self-respect and whatever courage is demanded, is to know where you yourself stand. That is, to have in words what you believe and are acting from.
William Faulkner

Conscience is the inner voice that warns us that someone might be looking.
H. L. Mencken

Politics have no relation to morals.
Niccolò Machiavelli

The path of least resistance leads to crooked rivers and crooked men.
Henry David Thoreau

But although denying that we have a special position in the natural world might seem becomingly modest in the eye of eternity, it might also be used as an excuse for evading our responsibilities. In our hands now lies not only our own future, but that of all living creatures with whom we share the earth.
David Attenborough

We must not, in trying to think about how we can make a big difference, ignore the small daily differences we can make which, over time, add up to big differences that we often cannot foresee.
Marian Wright Edelman

Right is right, even if everyone is against it; and wrong is wrong, even if everyone is for it.
William Penn

Excellence is an art won by training and habituation. We do not act rightly because we have virtue or excellence, but rather we have those because we have acted rightly. We are what we repeatedly do. Excellence, then, is not an act but a habit.
Aristotle

The world is not perishing for the want of clever, talented or well-meaning men. It is perishing for the want of men of courage and resolution.
Robert J. McCracken

The biggest need in politics and government today is for people of integrity and courage, who will do what they believe is right and not worry about the political consequences to themselves.
Reva Beck Bosone

I really wonder what gives us the right to wreck this poor planet of ours.
Kurt Vonnegut

What is wrong is never made right just because everyone is doing it. A bad idea is not made better just because a lot of people agree with it.
Ralph Marston

Treat the earth well: it was not given to you by your parents, it was loaned to you by your children. We do not inherit the Earth from our ancestors, we borrow it from our children.
Native American Indian Proverb

The power to do good is also the power to do harm.
Milton Friedman

Everyone thinks of changing the world, but no one thinks of changing himself.
Leo Tolstoy

Principle — particularly moral principle — can never be a weathervane, spinning around this way and that with the shifting winds of expediency. Moral principle is a compass forever fixed and forever true.
Edward R. Lyman

Whereas the truth can maintain itself forever, a deception can never stand on its own. Every dishonesty sets up a continuing drain on the resources of the person who engages in it.
Ralph Marston

Every act of dishonesty has at least two victims: the one we think of as the victim, and the perpetrator as well. Each little dishonesty makes another little rotten spot somewhere in the perpetrator's psyche.
Lesley Conger

There's an opportunity for businesses to demonstrate a role in society that is beyond profitability and shareholder value.
Howard Schultz

Every time we've made a decision to do the right thing it ends up being good business.
Yvon Chouinard

Every business has the potential for a higher purpose besides just making money.
John Mackey

Integrity is doing the right thing, even when no one is watching.
C. S. Lewis

I am free because I know that I alone am morally responsible for everything I do.
Robert A. Heinlein

The Sword of Truth is a blunt instrument without the keen edge of Justice.
Michael Rawls

It is not what we do, but also what we do not do, for which we are accountable.
Molière

If you find yourself planning to do something "just this once" watch out. It means you're about to compromise your own values. Whatever it is, you already know it's wrong.
Ralph Marston

Take responsibility for yourself...because no one's going to take responsibility for you.
Tyra Banks

The individual has always had to struggle to keep from being overwhelmed by the tribe. If you try it, you will be lonely often, and sometimes frightened. But no price is too high to pay for the privilege of owning yourself.
Friedrich Nietzsche

If it is not right, do not do it; if it is not true, do not say it.
Marcus Aurelius

Increase the space between stimulus and response, and your power to act on it with integrity. Pause, and then proactively choose a response that is deeply integrated with principles, needs, and capacities.
Stephen Covey

Character is what emerges from all the little things you were too busy to do yesterday, but did anyway.
Mignon McLaughlin

Your character will be what you yourself choose to make it.
John Lubbock

A business that makes nothing but money is a poor business.
Henry Ford

If, for any reason whatsoever, moral standards are conspicuously and unprecedentedly breached in one area of society, such as the political, it will follow as the night the day that those standards will start collapsing all down the line — in sports, entertainment, education, the armed forces, business, and government.
Margaret Halsey

You have to want to lose your appetite for violence or aggression. And to do that, you have to lose your self-righteousness.
Pema Chödrön

Few things can help an individual more than to place responsibility on him, and to let him know that you trust him.
Booker T. Washington

Any organization, in order to survive and achieve success, must have a sound set of beliefs on which it premises all its policies and actions.
Thomas J. Watson

Integrity is telling myself the truth. Honesty is telling the truth to other people.
Spencer Johnson

Live so that when your children think of fairness and integrity, they think of you.
H. Jackson Brown Jr.

Quality means doing it right when no one is looking.
Henry Ford

Integrity without knowledge is weak and useless, and knowledge without integrity is dangerous and dreadful.
Samuel Johnson

You cannot make yourself feel something you do not feel, but you can make yourself do right in spite of your feelings.
Pearl S. Buck

People with integrity do what they say they are going to do. Others have excuses.
Laura Schlessinger

Vulnerability sounds like truth and feels like courage. Truth and courage aren't always comfortable, but they're never weakness.
Brené Brown

In today's world I don't think corporations can only be focused on profits, because they are inextricably linked with the communities that they serve. I do not believe you can be a leader in your industry without being a leader in your community. It's a fundamental shift in how you think about business.
Marc Beinoff

There are no easy answers, but there are simple answers. We must have the courage to do what we know is morally right.
Ronald Reagan

When it comes to privacy and accountability, people always demand the former for themselves and the latter for everyone else.
David Brin

The ultimate measure of a man is not where he stands in moments of comfort, but where he stands at times of challenge and controversy.
Martin Luther King Jr.

Those companies unwilling to participate in improving and enhancing the communities they serve and the employees they employ will be in the penalty box. And they should be.
Howard Schultz

Surplus wealth is a sacred trust which its possessor is bound to administer in his lifetime for the good of the community.
Andrew Carnegie

The power of the Internet to change the world is real, but it is still up to mankind to change the world for the better.
Anthony Douglas Williams

When we fail to set boundaries and hold people accountable, we feel used and mistreated. This is why we sometimes attack who they are, which is far more hurtful than addressing a behavior or a choice.
Brené Brown

Leaders inspire accountability through their ability to accept responsibility before they place blame.
Courtney Lynch

It is not only what we do, but also what we do not do, for which we are accountable.
Molière

A body of men holding themselves accountable to nobody ought not to be trusted by anybody.
Thomas Paine

Most people do not really want freedom, because freedom involves responsibility, and most people are frightened of responsibility.
Sigmund Freud

Accountability is the measure of a leader's height.
Jeffrey Benjamin

Wisdom stems from personal accountability. We all make mistakes; own them...learn from them. Don't throw away the lesson by blaming others.
Steve Maraboli

The price of greatness is responsibility.
Winston Churchill

Responsibility equals accountability equals ownership. And a sense of ownership is the most powerful weapon a team or organization can have.
Pat Summitt

On good teams, coaches hold players accountable, on great teams players hold players accountable.
Joe Dumars

You can make any promises as long as you are not going to be there to fulfill them.
Pawan Mishra

Understanding the true meaning of accountability makes us strong and enables us to learn.
Sameh Elsayed

Restoring responsibility and accountability is essential to the economic and fiscal health of our nation.
Carl Levin

If you are building a culture where honest expectations are communicated and peer accountability is the norm, then the group will address poor performance and attitudes.
Henry Cloud

Good men are bound by conscience and liberated by accountability.
Wes Fessler

The only way we succeed as a group is not simply following directions, but in keeping each other accountable for our actions.
A. J. Darkholme

Accountability and self-responsibility are critical to our success in personal, professional and public life. However, we often look for those character traits in others, rather than inculcating them in ourselves.
Vishwas Chavan

You steadily grow into becoming your best as you choose to be accountable and accept responsibility for improvement.
Steve Shallenberger

Make yourself accountable and your employees will hold themselves to a high standard.
David J. Greer

Never promise more than you can perform.
Publilius Syrus

It is in your hands, to make a better world for all who live in it.
Nelson Mandela

Whenever you do a thing, act as if all the world were watching.
Thomas Jefferson

To see what is right and not do it is the want of courage.
Confucius

It is curious that physical courage should be so common in the world and moral courage so rare.
Mark Twain

I strongly believe the business of a business is to improve the world.
Marc Beinoff

The one thing that doesn't abide by majority rule is a person's conscience.
Harper Lee

I must admit that I personally measure success in terms of the contributions an individual makes to their fellow human beings.
Margaret Mead

Where there is no accountability, there will also be no responsibility.
Sunday Adelaja

We are a performance-driven organization, but we have to lead the company through the lens of humanity.
Howard Schultz

CHAPTER 9

Leadership Mindfulness

Leadership is a mental game. Part of being a great leader is being mentally strong, something that is not always easy when under pressure or when you are tired. Mindfulness, or the art of being present and acutely aware of your thoughts, emotions, and actions, is a great practice for monitoring your mental strength and emotional health.

Having core beliefs is another important factor in being mentally strong. That is why I place such important emphasis on having a Leadership Mindset based on your core beliefs (see chapter three).

Mindfulness is no longer just a New Age buzzword with no relevance to the rough and tumble world of business and leadership. Rather, this centuries-old practice of paying purposeful attention in the present moment without judgment is now being used by an ever-growing list of corporate leaders from Silicon Valley to Wall Street.

Mindfulness has been a hotbed topic of extensive scientific research in recent years, with much of the research revealing numerous physical and mental health-related benefits for those who engage in a regular mindfulness practice.

The many benefits for leaders of mindfulness include: greater attention, sharpened memory, improvement in complex thinking, better ability to analyze multiple sources of information, enriched listening skills, increased brain acuity, enhanced ability to remember faces and names, and heightened ability to read people's emotions.

Mindfulness is the practice of maintaining a nonjudgmental and heightened state of observation of your thoughts, emotions, and experiences at a particular moment in time. It is a capability that all humans possess.

The more often you can do this, the more consciously aware you become of the decisions you are making, the actions you are taking, and the behaviors you are exhibiting. Additionally, mindfulness helps interrupt automatic, reflexive reactions (both cognitive and emotional) that can lead to fear, worry, anxiety, angst, apprehension, and negative premonitions. By using mindfulness to our actual experiences in the moment we also increase the likelihood of exerting more conscious control over our reactions, thoughts, decisions, and behaviors.

The key is to be nonjudgmental in the moment. There's plenty of time later for rehashing how or why you have made a mistake, treated someone poorly, or done something that results in the carrying of some guilt or angst.

Mindfulness can also lead to an increased ability to break current habits holding you back from peak performance and inner peace. Additionally, just like our physical bodies, our brains can change its physical form and function throughout our lives in a process scientists call brain plasticity. And the best news: by using mindfulness practices and techniques you can be in charge of your brain and its future development.

While cognitive in approach, mindfulness goes beyond clarity and lucidness. Mindfulness results in greater confidence in one's actions and decisions, which means it is also a powerful way of battling that old foe procrastination. Those who are more confident in their decisions are more motivated to take action and be committed to pursuing desired outcomes than those who remain hesitant because their minds are too full for contemplative and calm analytical thoughts.

Stress Leads to Bad Decision Making

How does stress lead to bad decisions?

Neuroscience has revealed that as humans we rely on a pair of hardwired processes for decision making. Using pattern recognition our brains assess what appears to be going on. We then react to this information, or ignore it, due to the emotional tags stored in our memories. While normally highly reliable, these two processes can and do let us down, particularly in times of stress or tiredness.

In a process that scientists call pattern recognition, our brains try to reflexively counter decision-making anxieties by narrowing and simplifying our options. This attempt to find certainty in uncertain situations leads to premature conclusions that are often based on previous successful approaches and which prevents more and better options to surface or be considered.

In a similar way, emotional tagging in our memories sends us signals as to whether or not to pay attention to something or someone and what sort of action we should be considering. Interestingly, neurological research now shows that when the parts of our brain controlling emotions are damaged we become slow and incompetent decision makers even though we retain the capacity for objective analysis. We all know how it feels to make poor decisions when we are being "emotionally hijacked."

Usually, the more stressful the circumstances being faced are, the more a leader needs to explore a wide range of options and potential solutions. Unfortunately, while relying on past experiences may create a false sense of comfort and confidence, limiting one's options is more often than not a recipe for disaster and poor decision making.

Additionally, many poor decisions are made as a result of leaders feeling insecure about their positions, their career trajectories, their own confidence, and even what others may be thinking about them. Using mindfulness techniques and practices helps leaders remain mentally strong and capable of overcoming such insecurities.

Mindfulness has been proven to be a skillful way for stress reduction and all the associated ills and problems that result from accumulated stress. Additionally, stress reduction through mindfulness practices is a proven leadership performance advantage that comes with the side benefits of greater happiness, health, and wellbeing.

Another decision-making peril caused by stress is the tendency for leaders, particularly new supervisors and mid-level leaders to start (or increase) micromanaging. If this happens frequently it can have significant long-term negative consequences for their teams, as micromanaging is cited as one of the most common reasons employees quit. No one likes to be micromanaged by their leader.

To learn more about our one-day workshop *Better Decision Making: From Mind Full to Mindful Leadership Skills*, contact us via email: steven@CalienteLeadership.com

Leadership Mindfulness Is Not Passive

Leadership mindfulness is not a running away from difficult choices, a method for avoiding the reality of a situation, or even disengaging from the world and events around us.

Rather, mindfulness (and meditation as well) is a technique to calm and teach our minds a less reactionary way of handling emotions, situations, and decisions. By observing the ever-constant stream of thoughts and emotions that envelope us throughout the day, we are better positioned to be more contemplative, analytical, calm, and purposeful in our actions, decisions, and behaviors.

Mindfulness also enables leaders to be better at determining the complexity and interdependency of problems, identifying any unconscious biases that might be hidden in their decisions, and more cognizant of any emotions that might be swaying thoughts, decisions, actions, and behaviors.

Mindfulness is also a technique for being mentally strong in tough situations, thus aiding with resiliency, adaptability, hardiness, willpower, fortitude, and determination.

Amy Morin, author of *13 Things Mentally Strong People Don't Do*, has a list of the seven things mentally strong leaders know, all of which I would advocate are part of a leadership mindfulness mindset:

- It is important to admit when you do not have the answer.
- It is wise to acknowledge weaknesses, rather than waste energy masking vulnerabilities.
- There is always room for improvement.
- Character is more valuable than reputation.
- It is essential to pay attention to your emotions.
- The job of a leader is to control themselves, not other people.
- Struggles and tough times are opportunities to grow strong.

Mindfulness in the Workplace

It seems like every month there is new research coming out attesting to the efficacy of mindfulness in the workplace. Here are a few examples:

After more than 13,000 employees at Aetna took yoga and meditation sessions, they reported, on average, a 28% reduction in stress levels, a 20% improvement in sleep quality, and a 19% decrease in pain.

In 2013, a research study by Korn Ferry analysts David Zes and Dana Landis established a clear link between leader self-awareness and organizational performance after analyzing 486 companies and almost 7000 self-assessments of professionals within these firms. The researchers stated that *"public companies with a higher rate of return (ROI) also employ professionals who exhibit higher levels of self-awareness."*

A comprehensive study of mindfulness research, co-directed by a management scientist at Case Western Reserve University in 2016, came to the conclusion that *"injecting a corporate culture of mindfulness not only improves focus, but the ability to manage stress and how employees work together."*

An article in *Harvard Business Review* (December 2015) titled *How Meditation Benefits CEOs* covered a wide range of empirical research that has established the effectiveness of mindfulness strategies for the enhancement of resilience, emotional intelligence, empathy, creativity, and mental focus.

The self-awareness improvement from mindfulness is particularly useful for executives, as evidenced by the Korn Ferry research above. As Andy Lothian, CEO of Insights Learning and Development, pointed out in his article in *Training* (March/April 2017), *"It is individuals who lack self-awareness, especially those in leadership roles, who pose the real risk to organizational effectiveness."*

Of course, just as going for a single run will not create long-term health benefits, neither will one session of yoga or meditation create long-term brain health. You will need to commit to daily mindfulness practices to reap the scientifically-proven benefits being witnessed in both professional performance and personal life.

Quotes on Leadership Mindfulness

Act with purpose, courage, confidence, competence, and intelligence until these qualities "lock-in" to your subconscious mind.
Brian Tracy

You must learn a new way to think before you can master a new way to be.
Marianne Williamson

Don't let the noise of other's opinions drown out your own inner voice. And most important, have the courage to follow your heart and intuition. They somehow already know what you truly want to become. Everything else is secondary.
Steve Jobs

Nothing can harm you as much as your own thoughts unguarded.
Buddha

Freedom from the desire for an answer is essential to the understanding of a problem.
Jiddu Krishnamurti

There is more to life than increasing its speed.
Mohandas Karamchand (Mahatma) Gandhi

Peace of mind is attained not by ignoring problems, but by solving them.
Raymond Hull

Meditation is not evasion; it is a serene encounter with reality.
Thich Nhat Hanh

When we get too caught up in the busyness of the world, we lose connection with one another – and ourselves.
Jack Kornfield

Meditation practice isn't about trying to throw ourselves away and become something better. It's about befriending who we already are.
Pema Chödrön

We cannot force the development of mindfulness.
Allan Lokos

Open the window of your mind. Allow the fresh air, new lights, and new truths to enter.
Amit Ray

Step outside for a while – calm you mind. It is better to hug a tree than to bang your head against a wall continually.
Rasheed Ogunlaru

When you examine the lives of the most influential people who have ever walked among us, you discover one thread that winds through them all. They have been aligned first with their spiritual nature and only then with their physical selves.
Albert Einstein

Mindfulness means paying attention in a particular way: on purpose, in the present moment, and non-judgmentally. This kind of attention nurtures greater awareness, clarity, and acceptance of present-moment reality.
Jon Kabat-Zinn

The realization that you have control and influence over your own life is a key concept you will need to understand to practice mindfulness.
Janet Louise Stephenson

For peace of mind, resign as general manager of the universe.
Larry Eisenberg

The feeling that any task is a nuisance will soon disappear if it is done in mindfulness.
Thich Nhat Hanh

You cannot control the results, only your actions.
Allan Lokos

A few simple tips for life: feet on the ground, head to the skies, heart open, quiet mind.
Rasheed Ogunlaru

Is there a difference between happiness and inner peace? Yes. Happiness depends on conditions being perceived as positive; inner peace does not.
Eckhart Tolle

You'll never find peace of mind until you listen to your heart.
George Michael

Inward calm cannot be maintained unless physical strength is constantly and intelligently replenished.
Buddha

Contentment is an inexhaustible treasure.
Arabian Proverb

Relaxing in the midst of chaos, learning not to panic — this is the spiritual path.
Pema Chödrön

Being mindful means that we suspend judgment for a time, set aside our immediate goals for the future, and take in the present moment as it is rather than as we would like it to be.
Mark Williams

Essentially, meditation allows us to live in ways that are less automatic. This necessarily means less time spent worrying, ruminating, and trying to control things we can't control. It means we become less vulnerable to the throes of the fear-driven, older parts of our brains, and freer to use our newer and more sophisticated mental abilities: patience, compassion, acceptance, and reason.
David Cain

Peace comes from within. Do not seek it without.
Buddha

We often have very little empathy for our own thoughts and feelings and frequently try to suppress them by dismissing them as weaknesses.
Mark Williams

Wherever you are, be there totally.
Eckhart Tolle

The intuitive recognition of the instant, thus reality, is the highest act of wisdom.
David Suzuki

If you miss the present moment, you miss your appointment with life. That is very serious!
Thich Nhat Hanh

A mind beyond judgments watches and understands.
Buddha

I find that it is not the circumstances in which we are placed, but the spirit in which we face them, that constitutes our comfort.
Elizabeth T. King

He who would be serene and pure needs but one thing, detachment.
Meister Eckhart

To think bad thoughts is really the easiest thing in the world. If you leave your mind to itself it will spiral down into ever-increasing unhappiness. To think good thoughts, however, requires effort. This is one of the things that discipline — training —is about.
James Clavell

The most influential person who will talk to you all day is you, so you should be very careful about what you say to you!
Zig Ziglar

No matter how much pressure you feel at work, if you could find ways to relax for at least five minutes every hour, you'd be more productive.
Joyce Brothers

Start each day by affirming peaceful, contented, and happy attitudes and your days will tend to be pleasant and successful. Such attitudes are active and definite factors in creating satisfactory conditions. Watch your manner of speech then if you wish to develop a peaceful state of mind.
Norman Vincent Peale

Meditation is not a way of making your mind quiet. It's a way of entering into the quiet that's already there — buried under the 50,000 thoughts the average person thinks every day.
Deepak Chopra

Awareness is the greatest agent for change.
Eckhart Tolle

The key to success is to focus our conscious mind on things we desire not things we fear.
Brian Tracy

Thought is energy. Active thought is active energy; concentrated thought is a concentrated energy. Thought concentrated on a definite purpose becomes power.
Charles F. Haanel

Every experience, no matter how bad it seems, holds within it a blessing of some kind. The goal is to find it.
Buddha

It is only through your conscious mind that you can reach the subconscious. Your conscious mind is the porter at the door, the watchman at the gate. It is to the conscious mind that the subconscious looks for all its impressions.
Robert Collier

Nothing is a greater impediment to being on good terms with others than being ill at ease with yourself.
Honoré de Balzac

Whatever you believe with emotion becomes reality. You always act in a manner consistent with your innermost beliefs and convictions.
Brian Tracy

Breathing in I calm body and mind. Breathing out, I smile.
Thich Nhat Hahn

The emotions aren't always immediately subject to reason, but they are always immediately subject to action.
William James

You are what you think about all day long.
Robert Schuller

Just as your car runs more smoothly and requires less energy to go faster and farther when the wheels are in perfect alignment, you perform better when your thoughts, feelings, emotions, goals, and values are in balance.
Brian Tracy

Tension is who you think you should be. Relaxation is who you are.
Chinese Proverb

Mindfulness is the awareness that emerges through paying attention on purpose, in the present moment, and non-judgmentally, to things as they are.
Jon Kabat-Zinn

The only Zen you find on the tops of mountains is the Zen you bring up there.
Robert M. Pirsig

To think in terms of either pessimism or optimism oversimplifies the truth. The problem is to see reality as it is.
Thich Nhat Hanh

The only competition you will ever have is the competition between your disciplined and undisciplined mind.
James A. Ray

Our life is shaped by our mind, for we become what we think.
Buddha

When things are going wrong, take a breath and reset yourself. You do that through mindfulness — you just come right back in and collect yourself.
Phil Jackson

Peace of mind in the workplace is not the absence of conflict, but the ability to cope with it without drama or victimization.
Steven B. Howard

Meditation brings wisdom; lack of meditation leaves ignorance. Know well what leads you forward and what holds you back, and choose the path that leads to wisdom.
Buddha

If we are not fully ourselves, truly in the present moment, we miss everything.
Thich Nhat Hanh

Suffering usually relates to wanting things to be different than they are.
Allan Lokos

When you are present, you can allow the mind to be as it is without getting entangled in it.
Eckhart Tolle

Mindfulness isn't difficult, we just need to remember to do it.
Sharon Salzberg

Don't believe everything you think. Thoughts are just that – thoughts.
Allan Lokos

Mindfulness is simply being aware of what is happening right now without wishing it were different; enjoying the pleasant without holding on when it changes (which it will); being with the unpleasant without fearing it will always be this way (which it won't).
James Baraz

Mindfulness is the aware, balanced acceptance of the present experience. It isn't more complicated than that. It is opening to or receiving the present moment, pleasant or unpleasant, just as it is, without either clinging to it or rejecting it.
Sylvia Boorstein

The best way to capture moments is to pay attention. This is how we cultivate mindfulness. Mindfulness means being awake. It means knowing what you are doing.
Jon Kabat-Zinn

Life is a dance. Mindfulness is witnessing that dance.
Amit Ray

Let go of your mind and then be mindful. Close your ears and listen!
Rumi

If you concentrate on finding whatever is good in every situation, you will discover that your life will suddenly be filled with gratitude, a feeling that nurtures the soul.
Rabbi Harold Kushner

With our thoughts we make the world.
Buddha

Restore your attention or bring it to a new level by dramatically slowing down whatever you're doing.
Sharon Salzberg

Observe the space between your thoughts, then observe the observer.
Hamilton Boudreaux

The ability to be in the present moment is a major component of mental wellness.
Abraham Maslow

All action results from thought, so it is thoughts that matter.
Sai Baba

You cannot escape the results of your thoughts. Whatever your present environment may be, you will fall, remain or rise with your thoughts, your vision, your ideal. You will become as small as your controlling desire; as great as your dominant aspiration.
James Lane Allen

If you don't pay appropriate attention to what has your attention, it will take more of your attention than it deserves.
David Allen

In today's rush, we all think too much –seek too much – want too much – and forget about the joy of just being.
Eckhart Tolle

If the problem can be solved, why worry? If the problem cannot be solved worrying will do you no good.
Buddha

How you look at it is pretty much how you'll see it.
Rasheed Ogunlaru

If you want others to be happy, practice compassion. If you want to be happy, practice compassion.
Dalai Lama

If we learn to open our hearts, anyone, including the people who drive us crazy, can be our teacher.
Pema Chödrön

If the doors of perception were cleansed, everything would appear to man as it is, infinite.
William Blake

Feelings come and go like clouds in a windy sky. Conscious breathing is my anchor.
Thich Nhat Hanh

If you want to conquer the anxiety of life, live in the moment, live in the breath.
Amit Ray

You only lose what you cling to.
Buddha

You can't stop the waves, but you can learn to surf.
Jon Kabat-Zinn

A mind set in its ways is wasted.
Eric Schmidt

The mind is just like a muscle – the more you exercise it, the stronger it gets and the more it can expand.
Idowu Koyenikan

The stiller you are the calmer life is.
Rasheed Ogunlaru

One who is patient glows with an inner radiance.
Allan Lokos

Training your mind to be in the present moment is the #1 key to making healthier choices.
Susan Albers

Mindfulness practice means that we commit fully in each moment to be present; inviting ourselves to interface with this moment in full awareness, with the intention to embody as best we can an orientation of calmness, mindfulness, and equanimity right here and right now.
Jon Kabat-Zinn

CHAPTER 10

Leading Your Own Personal Development

T he biggest mistake new leaders make is thinking they already know everything they need to know in order to excel in their new leadership role.

However, the skills, knowledge, and experiences that create a successful and talented individual contributor are not necessarily transferable to the role of a leader. The truth is, you will never learn everything you need to know to be a great leader. Continuous learning and development are mandatory for continued leadership success.

For instance, you may know how to motivate yourself. But what motivates you is not necessarily what motivates any or all of your team members. The same applies to communication preferences. You may prefer delivering your messages orally, but some team members may need to see these in writing for them to understand and retain the information in them. This advice from Jedi Master Yoda is particularly relevant for new leaders, *"You must unlearn what you have learned."*

Your development as a leader will also come through experiences, especially difficult ones. As basketball coach Morgan Wooten has noted, *"You learn more from losing than winning. You learn to keep going."*

The art of great leadership requires a continuous evaluation and evolution of one's own leadership skills, mindset, philosophy, actions, and development.

All great leaders know that they need to continuously develop themselves. This is why taking charge and leading one's own personal and professional development is a core component of the art of great leadership.

Leading Self-Development

In chapter three we shared the importance of self-awareness and self-understanding in developing one's leadership mindset. These two qualities are equally important when it comes to your own self-development. For, as philosopher Baltasar Gracián wrote, *"Self-correction begins with self-knowledge."*

Learning to lead yourself, and your own professional development, reveals your values, non-negotiables, principles, and interests. This gives you direction and boundaries that will help keep you on course.

It also keeps you from leading people and teams to places you do not want to go or with methods you truly do not want to use.

Constantly thinking about and exploring the foundation of your leadership philosophy and mindset is also a core component of your on-going leadership development journey.

Think about it. Integrity, communicating, coaching, listening, providing feedback, delegation, influencing, motivating, and decision making may be called "soft skills," but they are the very skills you need to develop and grow as a leader. You don't want your team members to have only the same skills in three years as they do now. For the same reasons, you cannot afford to have only the same skills, capabilities, and competencies three years from now as you do today.

Additionally, as a leader you are in charge of your own self-development. You cannot afford to wait around for your talent development department or your human resources folks, or even your own manager, to create leadership development opportunities for you. When this does happen, take full advantage of such opportunities. But do not wait for such occasions to arise.

No leader should wait around for their manager to tell them how to develop as a leader. As April Arnzen, Senior Vice President of Human Resources at Micron Technology, tells her leaders throughout this Fortune 500 organization, *"Don't ever wait around for someone else to tell you how to develop yourself."* That's sage advice for leaders at any level of any organization.

Leadership Development Shortfalls

Where do leaders first learn their leadership skills?

Usually this comes from two sources: a) the leadership behaviors and actions of the bosses they have had throughout the early stages of their careers, and b) being thrown into the front lines of leadership with little more than expressions of confidence and best wishes by their managers.

Unfortunately, great individual contributors do not necessarily make good managers or great leaders. When promoted into supervisory or managerial roles, they tend to focus on the managerial aspects of processes, reporting, and executing what they are told.

As a result, they are totally unprepared for the critical leadership skills of coaching, providing feedback, increasing employee engagement, motivating team members, obtaining buy-in and commitment, fueling innovation, and generating new ideas.

Transitioning from a successful individual contributor role into a supervisory or manager position is fraught with challenges, concerns, and worries. This is a profound change with high risks of failure, personal dissatisfaction, team disenchantment, and even team member disengagement.

In many organizations, training is primarily focused on developing technical skills — creating managers and individual contributors who are functionally knowledgeable and competent in their respective jobs but who are not trained in the fundamentals of leading people.

One area of particular weakness in mid-level leaders and new supervisors that I have noticed in my 25 years of international leadership development training is their inability to give relevant, useful, and beneficial feedback. This inexperience and lack of expertise in proper feedback methodology significantly handicaps their ability to lead other team members.

Periods of high revenue growth often mask shortcomings in talent development, particularly within fast-growing small businesses and privately-owned companies. Gaps in existing leadership skills and competencies tend to go unnoticed when revenue is rapidly increasing year after year. It is only when growth suddenly declines that company owners and leaders become acutely aware of the significant shortfalls in leadership talent at all levels of the organization that is creating a bottleneck to continued growth.

Our best advice: don't let these leadership development shortfalls happen to you. Take charge of your own leadership development.

Your Leadership Development

Leadership development is a continuous journey. I know of no great leader who is not always on the lookout for new leadership ideas, techniques, and methodologies.

Fortunately, like any skill, leadership can be learned. And your proficiency in leadership can be improved through continuous practice and utilization of the leadership methods and tools you choose to use.

A key to developing your own personal leadership skills is to monitor your experiences, thoughts, and actions throughout the day. Research reported in *Harvard Business Review* (August 2017) showed that "leaders who are in learning mode develop stronger leadership skills than their peers."

A clear understanding of the current levels of one's various leadership skills is also critically important. But this does not mean you should be overly critical of your current skill levels or of any mistakes you make. It is far better to interpret a setback as evidence that you have not yet developed expertise in a particular skill than to allow a setback to convince you that you are not cut out to be a leader.

Three tips for building your leadership skills:

1) Focus on improvement over perfection. Don't lose sight of improvement by trying to become perfect at a particular skill. And give yourself credit when you have made improvements, even while knowing you still have room to improve.

2) Focus on process over results. One of my favorite advice to leaders applies to yourself as well: recognize effort, reward results. Keep your focus on the process of implementing a new skill and results will come.

3) Focus on the positives over negatives. We all tend to focus on what we need to improve, while forgetting to leverage the strengths of the skills we already have in place. Don't lose focus on what you are doing well and use these well-honed skills to build your other leadership skills.

By the way, these same three rules apply when you are helping team members or a colleague develop professionally.

Chances are you already know what leadership gaps you have, as well as what your leadership strengths are. The key to leveraging your strengths is through consistent behavior and actions. Purposeful action, based on your core leadership beliefs, prevents the handling of every situation you evaluate in an inconsistent, case-by-case manner.

Your leadership strengths can also be used to minimize or close any leadership skill gaps you have. Or at least buy you time to eliminate these gaps through coaching from others, your own reading and video research, or a formal classroom session.

My last advice is to approach your leadership development and learning journey with an open mind. Great leadership is an art, based on a core set of skills and behaviors you can learn.

Learning to lead others can feel enticing, alluring, exciting, and even satisfying. But learning to lead and develop yourself will feel powerful, empowered, aligned, confident, and authentically fulfilled.

Quotes on Leading Your Own Personal Development

A person who doesn't know, but knows that he doesn't know, is a student; teach him. A person who knows, but doesn't know that he knows, is asleep; awaken him. But a person who knows and knows that he knows is wise; follow him.
Chinese Proverb

You have to expect things of yourself before you can do them.
Michael Jordan

A growing body of research suggests that self-compassion, rather than self-esteem, may be the key to unlocking your true potential for greatness.
Heidi Grant Halvorson

Discipline is the bridge between goals and accomplishment.
Jim Rohn

Always remember you are braver than you believe, stronger than you seem, and smarter than you think.
Christopher Robin

It is your attitude, not your aptitude that determines your altitude.
Zig Ziglar

Visualize and think about yourself as you would ideally like to be, not just as you are.
Brian Tracy

The key to success is to keep growing in all areas of life — mental, emotional, spiritual, as well as physical.
Julius Erving

Self-correction begins with self-knowledge.
Baltasar Gracián

What is necessary to change a person is to change his awareness of himself.
Abraham Maslow

You are the only one holding you back.
Steven B. Howard

Don't ever wait around for someone else to tell you how to develop yourself.
April Arnzen

Be patient with yourself. Self-growth is tender; it's holy ground. There's no greater investment.
Stephen Covey

Desire is the starting point of all achievement.
Napoleon Hill

You are very powerful, provided you know how powerful you are.
Yogi Bhajan

The sages do not consider that making no mistakes is a blessing. They believe, rather, that the great virtue of man lies in his ability to correct his mistakes and continually make a new man of himself.
Wang Yang-Ming

Control your inner dialogue. Talk to yourself positively all the time.
Brian Tracy

Nothing so conclusively proves a man's ability to lead others as what he does from day to day to lead himself.
Thomas J. Watson

The greatest discovery of any generation is that human being can alter his life by altering his attitude.
William James

Motivation is a fire from within. If someone else tries to light that fire under you, chances are it will burn very briefly.
Stephen Covey

Motivation is what gets you started. Habit is what keeps you going.
Jim Rohn

Have a variety of interests. Interests relax the mind and lessen tension on the nervous system. People with many interests live not only longer but happier.
George Matthew Allen

We can often do more for others by trying to correct our own faults than by trying to correct theirs.
François Fénelon

Practice the philosophy of continuous improvement. Get a little bit better every single day.
Brian Tracy

The man who follows the crowd will usually get no further than the crowd. The man who walks alone is likely to find himself in places no one has ever been.
Alan Ashley-Pitt

The height of your accomplishments will equal the depth of your convictions.
William F. Scolavino

Real leaders forever need bigger and more irresistible challenges.
Mark Victor Hansen

Sometimes the most urgent thing you can possibly do is take a complete rest.
Ashleigh Brilliant

Feel the power that comes from focusing on what excites you.
Oprah Winfrey

Move out of your comfort zone. You can only grow if you are willing to feel awkward and uncomfortable when you try something new.
Brian Tracy

I was thinking one day and I realized that if I just had somebody behind me all the way to motivate me I could make a big difference. Nobody came along like that so I just became that person for myself.
Unknown

First we make our habits, then our habits make us.
Charles C. Noble

Let him that would move the world first move himself.
Socrates

He who knows others is learned; He who knows himself is wise.
Lao-Tzu

The world makes way for the man who knows where he is going.
Ralph Waldo Emerson

When you know yourself you are empowered. When you accept yourself you are invincible.
Tina Lifford

Be more concerned with your character than with your reputation. Your character is what you really are while your reputation is merely what others think you are.
John Wooden

You are your life's most important variable.
Steven B. Howard

Confidence without humility is arrogance.
Unknown

Always give without remembering, and always receive without forgetting.
Brian Tracy

The elevator to success is out of order. You'll have to use the stairs, one step at a time.
Joe Girard

Always bear in mind that your own resolution to succeed is more important than any other one thing.
Abraham Lincoln

Argue for your limitations, and sure enough, they're yours.
Johann Sebastian Bach

What we see depends mainly on what we look for.
John Lubbock

Treat your body like a temple, not a woodshed. The mind and body work together. Your body needs to be a good support system for the mind and spirit. If you take good care of it, your body can take you wherever you want to go, with the power and strength and energy and vitality you will need to get there.
Jim Rohn

The health of your body influences what you experience in your mind. There is no split. If you can engage your whole spirit in the pursuit of total fitness — not just your intellect, not just your emotions — but instead everything inside you that is truly you, you'll discover what it is to be a whole person.
David Patchell-Evans

It is not work that kills men; it is worry. Work is healthy; you can hardly put more upon a man than he can bear. Worry is rust upon the blade. It is not the revolution that destroys the machinery, but the friction. Fear secretes acids; but love and trust are sweet juices.
Henry Ward Beecher

Personality development is the process of building and maintaining high levels of self-esteem. You can change your performance by changing the way you think about yourself in that area.
Brian Tracy

Laughter is the most healthful exertion.
Christoph Wilhelm Hufeland

Try not to become a man of success, but rather try to become a man of value.
Albert Einstein

Whether you be man or woman you will never do anything in this world without courage. It is the greatest quality of the mind next to honor.
James Lane Allen

Miss a meal if you have to, but don't miss a book.
Jim Rohn

Read an hour every day in your chosen field. This works out to about one book per week, 50 books per year, and will guarantee your success.
Brian Tracy

Read something positive every night and listen to something helpful every morning.
Tom Hopkins

The ability to concentrate and to use time well is everything.
Lee Iacocca

Take the time to concentrate. Put your mind through an enjoyable, strenuous workout and feel the power as your mental muscles grow ever stronger.
Ralph Marston

Focus on your potential instead of your limitations.
Alan Loy McGinnis

Preconceived notions are the locks on the door to wisdom.
Merry Browne

Those who think they have not time for bodily exercise will sooner or later have to find time for illness.
Edward Stanley

The book you don't read won't help.
Jim Rohn

When I let go of what I am, I become what I might be.
Lao-Tzu

Make a strong commitment to reach your full potential as a human being.
Nido Qubein

You can make more friends in two months by becoming interested in other people than you can in two years by trying to get other people interested in you.
Dale Carnegie

Make a total commitment to your company, your job, and your career. Uncommitted people have no future.
Brian Tracy

What you commit yourself to determines what you are, more than anything that ever happened to you yesterday, or the day before.
Anthony Campolo

Fear less, hope more, eat less, chew more, whine less, breathe more, talk less, say more, hate less, love more, and good things will be yours.
Swedish Proverb

One characteristic of winners is they always look upon themselves as a do-it-yourself project.
Denis Waitley

We must always change, renew, rejuvenate ourselves, otherwise we harden.
Johann Wolfgang von Goethe

If you take responsibility for yourself you will develop a hunger to accomplish your dreams.
Les Brown

The illiterate of the 21st century will not be those who cannot read and write, but those who cannot learn, unlearn, and relearn.
Alvin Toffler

The depth of your belief and the strength of your conviction determines the power of your personality.
Brian Tracy

To succeed in life, you need three things: a wishbone, a backbone and a funny bone.
Reba McEntire

Be who you are and say what you feel, because those who mind don't matter, and those who matter don't mind.
Dr. Seuss

Reading is essential for those who seek to rise above the ordinary. We must not permit anything to stand between us and the book that could change our lives.
Jim Rohn

Most people have no idea of the giant capacity we can immediately command when we focus all of our resources on mastering a single area of our lives.
Anthony Robbins

Observe and Absorb.
Steven B. Howard

Confidence comes not from always being right but from not fearing to be wrong.
Peter T. McIntyre

There is no paycheck that can equal the feeling of contentment that comes from being the person you are meant to be.
Oprah Winfrey

A creative man is motivated by the desire to achieve, not by the desire to beat others.
Ayn Rand

The distance between who I am and who I want to be is separated only by my actions and words.
Anonymous

If we're growing, we're always going to be out of our comfort zone.
John Maxwell

In this world you're either growing or you're dying so get in motion and grow.
Lou Holtz

Every moment of one's existence one is growing into more or retreating into less.
Norman Mailer

We cannot become what we want to be by remaining where we are.
Max De Pree

If you put yourself in a position where you have to stretch outside your comfort zone, then you are forced to expand your consciousness.
Les Brown

To the degree we're not living our dreams, our comfort zone has more control of us than we have over ourselves.
Peter McWilliams

One can choose to go back toward safety or forward toward growth. Growth must be chosen again and again; fear must be overcome again and again.
Abraham Maslow

It is not because things are difficult that we do not dare, it is because we do not dare that they are difficult.
Seneca

Low self-esteem is like driving through life with your handbrake on.
Maxwell Maltz

Learning is weightless, a treasure you can always carry easily.
Chinese Proverb

The ability to seek out information and take ownership of your own learning is far more important than any particular skill.
Salman Khan

I've always felt it was not up to anyone else to make me give my best.
Hakeem Olajuwon

Don't be a prisoner of your past. Be the architect of your future.
Steven B. Howard

Develop your willpower so that you can make yourself do what you should do, when you should do it, whether you feel like it or not.
Brian Tracy

The bad news is time flies. The good news is you're the pilot.
Michael Altshuler

First you form your habits, and then your habits form you. Make the investment in your own positive habits, and you could well enjoy the dividends throughout your entire life.
Ralph Marston

Stand apart from your dreams. Look at them. Write about them. Wrestle with them until you're convinced they're based on principles that will bring results. Then use your creative imagination to explore new applications, new ways of doing things that have the principle-based power to translate dreaming into doing.
Stephen Covey

The ability to learn is the most important quality a leader can have.
Sheryl Sandberg

There is no cure and no improving of the world that does not begin with the individual himself.
Carl Jung

As you become more clear about who you really are, you'll be better able to decide what is best for you the first time around.
Oprah Winfrey

Reduce your plan to writing. The moment you complete this, you will have definitely given concrete form to the intangible desire.
Napoleon Hill

Write your goals down in detail and read your list of goals every day. This will keep your subconscious mind focused on what you want step by step.
Jack Canfield

Communication is a skill that you can learn. It's like riding a bicycle or typing. If you're willing to work at it, you can rapidly improve the quality of every part of your life.
Brian Tracy

When you are content to be simply yourself and don't compare or compete, everybody will respect you.
Lao-Tzu

To help others develop, start with yourself! When the boss acts like a little god and tells everyone else they need to improve, that behavior can be copied at every level of management. Every level then points out how the level below it needs to change. The end result: no one gets much better.
Marshall Goldsmith

The more seriously you take your growth, the more seriously your people will take you.
John Maxwell

Accept no one's definition of your life, but define yourself.
Harvey Fierstein

When you write down your ideas you automatically focus your full attention on them. Few if any of us can write one thought and think another at the same time. Thus a pencil and paper make excellent concentration tools.
Michael Leboeuf

The greatest danger for most of us is not that we aim too high and we miss it, but that our aim is too low and we reach it.
Michaelangelo

Steven Howard's Personal Leadership Philosophy

L eadership is an art.

It is the art of achieving progress through the involvement and actions of others.

The best leaders are people who lead from their own personal strengths, leadership philosophy, and leadership mindset. Great leaders also understand that organizational energy, workplace synergy, and end results are best attained when ambitious people with different and diverse backgrounds and thinking preferences are allowed to perform work together in a safe and supportive environment.

Successful leaders know how to create such thriving and supportive climates by applying the skills of adaptability, motivation, coaching, focus, collaboration, decision-making, communications, and personal development to both themselves and the people they lead.

Strong leaders leverage the emotions of passion, enthusiasm, self-satisfaction, trust, and loyalty to drive creativity, thinking, innovation, energy, and buy-in to strategies, tactics, and activities in pursuit of clearly stated goals and objectives.

Steven Howard's Rules of Great Leadership

1. Leadership is about both people and results. If you have to neglect one, neglect the results for these will come in time when you have developed your people.

2. Great leaders are great listeners. They know they learn more from listening than from speaking.

3. Great leadership happens at all levels of an organization, not just in the executive suites or ownership ranks.

4. People development is the single most important long-term priority and responsibility of all leaders, at all levels of an organization. Great leaders ensure that this happens.

5. Great leaders are made through circumstances, experiences, reflection, and skill enhancement.

6. Great leadership is honed by reflection, mindfulness, compassion, and action. It is enhanced via continuous learning and improvement.

7. When great leadership is exhibited at all levels of an organization, competitive advantage ensues.

8. Great leaders create more leaders, not just followers.

9. Great leaders know they cannot lead everyone. Some people may not want to be led by them. When this happens agree to go your separate ways respectfully.

10. Great leadership is achieving results through others while enhancing the skills and talents of team members.

11. A focus on people development is one of the most important factors that differentiates great leaders from good leaders.

12. Great leaders practice Leadership Accountability, holding themselves and other leaders accountable for their leadership behaviors, actions, and for making ethical decisions.

13. Great leaders give team members a sense of purpose and a compelling context for committing to buy-in.

14. Great leaders give team members appropriate levels of autonomy and authority.

15. Great leaders create a safe environment where mistakes are tolerated (and learned from) and where accountability is fair and unbiased.

16. Great leaders devote significant energy and time clarifying and understanding the perspectives, ideas, concerns, and questions of others.

17. Great leaders do not see clarification questions from team members and peers as push-back.

18. Great leaders assert their right to express their viewpoints, concerns, and questions to senior leaders and team members in a professional and respectful manner.

19. Great leaders show empathy to team members by understanding the emotions and feelings they are going through, particularly during times of change.

20. The leadership behaviors of great leaders are almost always fully congruent with their self-understood and deeply believed leadership philosophy and leadership mindset. Any incongruences are usually the exceptions that prove the rule.

21.   Everyone needs a code they can lead by. That is why great leaders have their own written leadership philosophy that strongly influences how they interpret reality and guides them on how to react to people, events, and situations.

About the Author

S teven Howard is an award-winning author of 19 books and when he is not writing specializes in creating and delivering Leadership Development programs for frontline leaders, mid-level leaders, supervisors, senior leaders, and high-potential leaders.

He has 38 years of international senior sales, marketing, and leadership experience. His corporate career covered a wide variety of fields and experiences, including Regional Marketing Director for Texas Instruments Asia-Pacific, Regional Director (South Asian & ASEAN) for TIME Magazine, Global Account Director at BBDO Advertising handling an international airline account, and Vice President Marketing for Citibank's Consumer Banking Group.

Since 1993 he has delivered leadership development programs in the U.S., Asia, Australia, New Zealand, Fiji, Canada, Africa, Arabian Gulf, and Europe to numerous organizations, including Citicorp, Covidien, Danaher, DBS Bank, Deutsche Bank, DuPont Lycra, Esso Productions, ExxonMobil, Hewlett Packard, Imerys, Irving Oil, Micron Technology, Motorola Solutions, SapientNitro, Shire Pharmaceuticals, Standard Chartered Bank, and others.

He has been a member of the training faculty at MasterCard University Asia/Pacific, the Citibank Asia-Pacific Banking Institute, and Forum Corporation. He brings a truly international, cross-cultural perspective to his leadership development programs, having lived in the USA for 28 years, in Singapore for 21 years, and in Australia for 12 years.

In addition to his leadership facilitation work, Steven has served on several Boards in both the private and non-profit sectors. He has also chaired a strategic advisory group for a local government entity and a national sporting organization that is a member of the Australian Olympic Committee.

Steven is the author of 19 leadership, marketing, and management books and the editor of nine professional and personal development books in the *Project You* series.

His other books are:

8 Keys to Becoming a Great Leader: *With leadership lessons and tips from Gibbs, Yoda & Capt'n Jack Sparrow*

Leadership Lessons from the Volkswagen Saga

Asian Words of Success

Indispensable Asian Words of Knowledge

Asian Words of Inspiration

Asian Words of Meaning

The Book of Asian Proverbs

Marketing Words of Wisdom

The Best of the Monday Morning Marketing Memo

Powerful Marketing Memos

Corporate Image Management: A Marketing Discipline

Powerful Marketing Minutes: 50 Ways to Develop Market Leadership

MORE Powerful Marketing Minutes: 50 New Ways to Develop Market Leadership

Asian Words of Wisdom

Asian Words of Knowledge

Essential Asian Words of Wisdom

Pillars of Growth: Strategies for Leading Sustainable Growth (co-author with three others)

Motivation Plus Marketing Equals Money (co-author with four others)

Contact Details

Email: steven@CalienteLeadership.com

Twitter: @stevenbhoward | @GreatLeadershp

LinkedIn: www.linkedin.com/in/stevenbhoward

Facebook: www.facebook.com/CalienteLeadership

Website: www.CalienteLeadership.com

Blog: CalienteLeadership.com/TheArtofGreatLeadershipBlog

Made in the USA
Las Vegas, NV
15 March 2021